PICTURE HISTORY OF EARLY AVIATION

1903–1913

Joshua Stoff

DOVER PUBLICATIONS, INC. • NEW YORK

For Jill, Matthew and Tyler
all of whom make life worth living . . .

PHOTO CREDITS: All photographs marked "CAM" are from the collection of the Cradle of Aviation Museum, Garden City, New York. All photographs marked "NASM" are from the collection of the National Air and Space Museum, Smithsonian Institution, Washington, D.C.

Copyright

Published in Canada by General Publishing Company, Ltd., 30 Lesmill Road, Don Mills, Toronto, Ontario.
Published in the United Kingdom by Constable and Company, Ltd., 3 The Lanchesters, 162–164 Fulham Palace Road, London W6 9ER.

Bibliographical Note

Picture History of Early Aviation, 1903–1913, is a new work, first published by Dover Publications, Inc., in 1996.

Edited by Alan Weissman

Book design by Jeanne Joudry

Library of Congress Cataloging-in-Publication Data

Stoff, Joshua.
    Picture history of early aviation, 1903–1913 / Joshua Stoff.
        p.   cm.
    Includes index.
    ISBN 0-486-28836-6 (pbk.)
    1. Aeronautics—History.   2. Airplanes—Pictorial works.   I. Title.
TL515.S864   1995
629.13'009—dc20
                                                                    95-44658
                                                                    CIP

Manufactured in the United States of America
Dover Publications, Inc., 31 East 2nd Street, Mineola, N.Y. 11501

CONTENTS

INTRODUCTION

To fly like the birds has always been a dream of mankind. The very idea of flight has always intrigued us. Today, although we rarely think twice about ascending in a Boeing 747—for the cost of only an airline ticket—when we *do* think about it, the idea of so enormous an object rising from the ground and flying under its own power can still strike us with awe. Awe of this kind inspired countless attempts over the centuries to emulate the birds. Every one of these attempts ended in dismal failure—until approximately 10:35 A.M. Eastern Standard Time, December 17, 1903.

At that moment, Orville Wright's amazing twelve-second flight over the sand dunes near Kitty Hawk, North Carolina, seemed to break an age-old spell that had prevented man from conquering the air. Quickly, scientists, tinkerers, daredevils, inventors and mechanics all plunged headlong into the great adventure. Now triumph was followed by triumph—and often by spectacular failure. For modern achievements in aviation did not come without great cost, and both lives and fortunes were lost.

In adventure and excitement, in romance and color, the first decade of flight after Kitty Hawk in many ways remains the most dramatic of all. It is true that, for nearly five years, things remained quiet. But then, inspired by the Wright brothers' public demonstrations in 1908 and 1909, French aviators and airplane designers made up for lost time. Although in this period the Americans and also the British continued to be worthy contenders for honors, it was the French who took the lead in aeronautical achievements. Latham, Paulhan and many others quickly established themselves as heroes of the air, and designer-manufacturers like Farman and Levavasseur came up with unusual planes of types very different from anything even the ingenious Americans had thought of.

Most outstanding of all was Louis Blériot, who amazed the world with his spectacular hop across the English Channel, on July 25, 1909. This was the first notable long-distance flight, and crowds on both sides of the Channel expressed their frenetic appreciation much as similar crowds would react to Lindbergh's trans-Atlantic crossing eighteen years later.

Accustomed as we are now to safety in the air, when flying around the world is safer than driving to a nearby grocery, it is hard to keep in mind how dangerous flying was in those early days. For the first thirty years or so, nearly all airplanes were fragile-looking wooden structures braced by wires and covered with varnished fabric. The structural material of choice was spruce, a strong, light, straight-grained wood, not prone to splitting. The most favored covering was finely woven linen. Second-most favored was cotton, which could not be woven as tight. After being stitched onto the framework, the fabric was brushed with a cellulose varnish known as "dope." This sealed the fabric's pores, making it airtight, and also shrank its threads to make a strong, taut covering.

Until the end of World War I, aircraft propellers were almost always carved from solid blocks of wood—walnut, oak or ash. Altogether, aside from the engine and fasteners, these early aircraft had very little metal in them, and in fact could be said to be a collection of vegetable products! This was understandable since the only engines available were grossly inefficient for their weight. After a designer had selected the lightest and most powerful engine he could find (or at least the best he could afford), he had to do the best he could to save weight in the airplane itself.

The odd appearance of early aircraft also comes from the fact that little was known about aerodynamics in the early years of this century, and no one had yet determined what configuration an efficient airplane should have. That is why pre–World War I aircraft had as many designs as designers. Furthermore, the external bracing struts and wires required by these frail aircraft generated so much drag that early aviators were forced to hobble through the air at speeds under 55 mph. Gradually, as aviators were forced to fly faster to win contests, the external form of the airplane was simplified and streamlined.

Also a matter for lively debate in the early years of powered flight was the relative superiority of monoplanes and biplanes. Even now, we may well ask, Why *were* there so many biplanes among the early flying machines? As proponents of the monoplane at the time noted, there are no biplanes in nature: all birds are monoplanes. The answer to this question is a matter of wing loading, wing area and structural integrity. Early aircraft were heavy relative to their power. Therefore, to avoid excessive wing loading (the weight carried by each square foot of wing surface) early airplane designers had to design the wings to have as much surface as possible. Excess wing loading requires a plane to be flown and landed at inordinately high speeds just to keep it from stalling and falling out of the sky. A biplane configuration yields twice as much wing surface for a given wingspan as a monoplane. Early monoplanes required very long wings to achieve low wing loading, and such structures were heavy, clumsy and difficult to brace properly, especially given the engineering techniques of the day. The wings of a biplane, secured by struts and braced by wires (much like a bridge), formed an inherently strong structure. There was a price to pay—greater aerodynamic drag—but until about 1930 this was considered acceptable in return for greater structural integrity.

Even the safest planes of those pioneering days were, relative to today's, death traps. To leave the safety of Mother Earth on those frail wings, and climb into the sky, an unexplored element into which the pioneers of flight knew they were penetrating only at great risk, demanded a unique blend of courage, dedication, curiosity and fanaticism. These qualities linked the early aviators—and there were not really that many of them—into a single brotherhood (and sisterhood, since a surprising number were women), accepting a common challenge. Whatever their country of origin, they practically all knew one another. Although there were intense rivalries among them, there was really little jealousy: each knew what the others were up against. When one failed and was killed, the survivors felt deeply the loss of a fellow pioneer who would seek the skies no more. In a few brief years, all this would change. During the course of World War I, the frail doves would become menacing birds of prey, and the first aviators, once united by a common bond, suddenly found themselves enemies, shooting at each other, albeit reluctantly, in the skies over France. A certain innocence had been lost, and from then on there were two types of aviation: flying for war and flying for peace.

For a few glorious years before this, however, beginning around 1910, flying fever infected people everywhere. An elite band of pioneering aviators emerged as the international heroes of their day, more celebrated than any of today's sports stars or rock idols. Their names became household words, immortalized on souvenirs, posters and postcards, and the newspapers carried daily messages recording their marvelous exploits as they competed for huge prizes in air races and earned incredible fees for exhibitions. These rewards motivated them to push their frail craft to their limits of altitude, speed and endurance.

Now, decades later, we may read of the adventures and conquests of the first aviators and be proud of their perseverance and accomplishments. For, taking enormous risks and often making the supreme sacrifice, these pioneers played a crucial role in taking what had begun as little more than a motorized box kite and transforming it into an integral and essential part of everyday life in the twentieth century. Here, in words and pictures, is their story.

PICTURE HISTORY OF EARLY AVIATION

1903–1913

PIONEERS

1

1 The dominant figure in aeronautics in the decade immediately preceding powered flight was Otto Lilienthal, born in Germany in 1848. Lilienthal tackled the problem of human flight in a scientific way. Understanding the supreme importance in human flight of an effective wing, between 1891 and 1896 Lilienthal built and flew a series of gliders that incorporated superior wings and thus were the most successful aircraft yet built (though of course still unpowered). He built several different man-carrying gliders and test-flew them himself from a 150-foot-high man-made hill near Berlin. (NASM)

2 Lilienthal's gliders were made of a willow frame covered with tightly stretched fabric. Most, like this one, were monoplanes, although he also experimented with biplanes. At a time when powered "aircraft" could do no more than lumber along the ground, Lilienthal's machines were making glides of over a thousand feet. They were controlled by the pilot's shifting his weight, as in a modern hang glider. (NASM)

3 Here is Lilienthal ready to launch his glider. During a glide like this one, on August 9, 1896, soon after this picture was taken, a sudden gust of wind threw Lilienthal's glider off balance. He was unable to recover and he plummeted to his death. Although Lilienthal's research had probably already taken him as far as he could go, and his gliders were unstable and had other severe limitations, he had nevertheless made a major contribution to research on heavier-than-air flight. His writings, translated and read throughout the world, demonstrated the likelihood that further work would in fact lead to the reality of a flying machine, and, thus, many others were inspired to continue where Lilienthal left off. (NASM)

2

4 In America, Langley, Chanute and the Wright brothers, all present or future experimenters in human flight, were inspired by the photos of Lilienthal flying on artificial wings. Several copies of Lilienthal gliders were built and flown in the United States. One glider actually built by Lilienthal himself was purchased by William Randolph Hearst and brought to New York. It was apparently flown several times on Long Island and Staten Island in the late 1890s. Shown in this photo on exhibit at the first aeronautical exhibition in New York City in 1906, this device, amazingly, has survived and is now at the National Air and Space Museum in Washington. (CAM)

5 After Lilienthal's death, the bearer of the torch of aeronautical progress appeared in the United States in the unlikely form of an aging civil engineer named Octave

Chanute. Born in Paris in 1832 and arriving in this country with his parents six years later, Chanute did not become interested in aeronautics until 1889, after a successful career building railroads and bridges. Soon Chanute knew more about the history of man's attempts to fly than anyone on earth. In 1894 he published the seminal work *Progress in Flying Machines*. This book, fully documenting the history of aviation to that time, became a Bible for anyone attempting further research in the field. Chanute developed his own biplane gliders and had them test-flown at Indian Dunes Park near Lake Michigan, outside Chicago, in 1896 and 1897. These experiments were successful and convinced Chanute that it was possible to build an inherently stable craft that could maintain its balance in the air without gyrations by the pilot. (NASM)

5

4

6

7

6, 7 Among the several aeronautical enthusiasts who were eager to work for Chanute was Augustus Herring, a resident of Long Island, New York, who had already built and flown a Lilienthal-type glider. These photos show him flying this glider in the Bronx, New York, in 1894. The following year he moved to Chicago in order to work directly with Chanute. (CAM)

8

8 Herring at Indian Dunes with a Chanute-type glider of his own construction, in 1896. This craft, weighing only 23 pounds, had a combination rudder and stabilizer in the tail. Nevertheless, stability and control were achieved primarily by the pilot's shifting of his weight. (CAM)

9 The Chanute-Herring glider in flight at Indian Dunes. This machine made many glides of over 300 feet and had a pleasantly gradual rate of descent. In the fall of 1896, Chanute and Herring, pleased with its performance, offered free rides to visitors, several of whom accepted the offer and made successful flights in it. After this, Chanute and Herring split up. Chanute felt that more work was needed with gliders before attempting a powered flight, whereas Herring wanted to move on immediately. (CAM)

9

10

11

12

10 Herring's powered flying machine being tested on the beach at St. Joseph, Michigan, before several eyewitnesses on October 11, 1898. After Herring started the engine and ran with it for several steps, this craft actually lifted into the air and flew for about 60 feet. Although Herring did become airborne in this machine, it is still not considered to have achieved true heavier-than-air flight, as the flight could be neither sustained nor controlled—essential factors in truly practical powered flight. Nevertheless the problem of achieving such flight now seemed much closer to solution. (CAM)

11 Percy Pilcher flying one of his gliders in the 1890s. A Scotsman, Pilcher was inspired by Lilienthal in 1895. He at first worked with Lilienthal and then began building the *Hawk*, a glider of his own design with improvements such as cambered wings, a hinged tail unit and a wheeled undercarriage. With this device he was able to make glides of up to 750 feet. In 1899 Pilcher built a powered version of this glider. Before he could test it he was killed in a gliding crash on September 30 of that year. (NASM)

12 Working in Connecticut at the turn of the century, mechanic Gustave Whitehead, a German immigrant, built several flying machines along novel lines. In the machine shown in this photograph, Whitehead claimed to have flown over a mile on August 14, 1901. He never had a successful public demonstration, however, and in fact it is doubtful that this machine ever flew at all. Whitehead was one of many experimenters who, despite claims to the contrary—and perhaps having worked genuinely hard with every good intention—contributed nothing at all to the progress of aviation. (NASM)

13 As early as 1884, John Montgomery of California was flying a glider with a curved wing and rear stabilizer, like the one in this picture. He soon progressed to a tandem-wing device that was released from a balloon at four thousand feet and glided down from there. Although Montgomery's contribution to aviation was minimal, he has been called "The Father of Basic Flying." (NASM)

14 Several exhibition flights were made with the Montgomery glider by daredevil Dan Maloney in California in 1905, as seen here. Maloney claimed to be able to control the glider by moving wires attached to the wings, a crude form of wing warping, the control method used by the Wright brothers. Maloney was killed in a glider crash in 1905; Montgomery died the same way in 1911. (NASM)

13

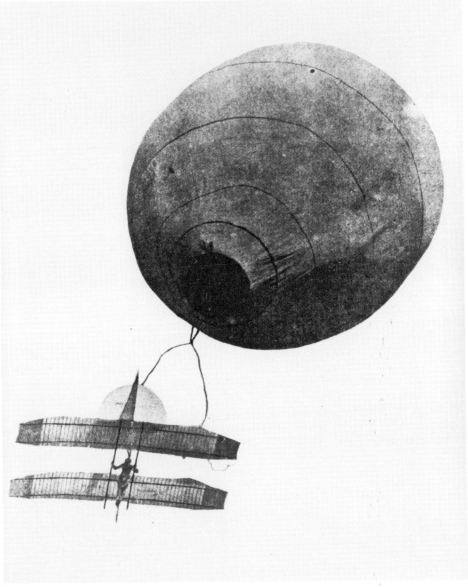

14

15

16

17

15   The Aeronautic Society of New York was founded in 1908 with the purpose of pooling the members' resources and ideas in the pursuit of the problem of mechanical flight by man. This organization was among the first such in the world to have its own flying grounds, workshops and hangars. Their first headquarters, established in 1908, was at the Morris Park Race Track in the Bronx. In this photo member Lawrence Lesh is seen at Morris Park in his glider, being towed by an automobile. (CAM)

16   In 1909 the Aeronautic Society of New York moved to Long Island, where many of its members lived. Here is Tom Kramer's glider being towed aloft by an automobile at Oceanside, Long Island, in 1909. (CAM)

17   The glider of Aeronautic Society member Henry Newell, built by him and his brother William, and flown by Henry, seen here, in Richmond Hill, Queens, 1909. (CAM)

18   Hiram Stevens Maxim, born in Maine in 1840, used much of the proceeds from his successful development of the machine gun to experiment in aeronautics. By this time, the late 1880s, he had settled in England (he was later naturalized as a British subject). Maxim began from scratch, paying no attention to developments elsewhere. He used his own whirling-arm device and wind tunnel to test wing shapes. In 1893 he built a gigantic man-carrying biplane with a wingspan of 105 feet and two steam engines driving two eighteen-foot-long propellers. There were monoplane elevators fore and aft. Steering was possible by separately controlling the two steam engines. This monster weighed in at 8,000 pounds (by contrast, the Wright brothers' first powered machine weighed only 650 pounds). When Maxim's machine was tested on a special 200-foot-long track, on July 31, 1894, it was supposed to remain under the constraint of special guard rails. Unfortunately, it didn't. It succeeded in rising off the ground, but then fouled an upper guide

rail and crashed to one side. Unable to afford to repair the extensive damage, Maxim abandoned the development of his flying machine. (CAM)

19   Another pioneer of early flight was Professor Samuel Pierpont Langley, born in Massachusetts in 1834. A distinguished astrophysicist, in 1887 he became Secretary of the Smithsonian Institution (a position he held until his death in 1906). With a strong belief in the feasibility of mechanical flight, in 1891 Langley began to experiment in aeronautics, both in the laboratory and by the building of models. By 1896 he had built a number of 14-foot-wingspan steam-powered models (like the one in this photo) that, launched from his houseboat on the Potomac River, made a remarkable series of flights. Model No. 6 flew under its own power for an amazing 4,800 feet on November 28 of that year. These experiments marked the first time any man-made heavier-than-air machine had achieved free, sustained flight. (NASM)

18

19

20

21

23

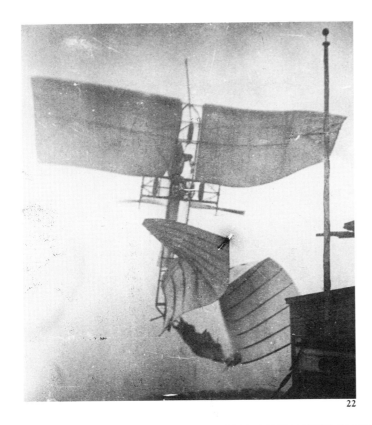

22

24

25

20 In 1897 Langley felt he had established the feasibility of heavier-than-air mechanical flight and would leave further research—including that with man-carrying machines—for others. He was nevertheless encouraged to pursue work with a man-carrying version of his plane when he received a War Department grant of $50,000 in 1898 for such a project. Despite all the resources available to him as head of the Smithsonian, it took Langley five years to have a suitable lightweight gasoline engine built for his machine. The engine, a remarkable feat of engineering, was built for him by his chief engineer and pilot, Charles Manly. Finally, on October 8, 1903, his *Aerodrome*, with Manly at the controls, was ready for catapult-launching from his houseboat, as seen here. (NASM)

21 Despite the most careful preparations, on being launched, the *Aerodrome* was snagged by the launching mechanism. It was pitched down so steeply that Manly could not recover it, and the plane plunged into the Potomac. Manly was lucky to escape the wreckage, which was salvaged for repair. (NASM)

22 On December 8, 1903, when Langley's funds were exhausted and he was being ridiculed by the press, his rebuilt *Aerodrome* stood once again on the roof of the houseboat for one last try at man-carrying, powered flight. At 4:45 P.M., the catapult shot the machine off the end of the houseboat. Immediately it flipped on end and folded in half, as captured in this photo. Again the wreckage ended up in the Potomac, and Manly was lucky to escape. There would be no third try. Stung by ridicule in the press, Langley would experiment in aeronautics no more. The disaster seemed only to demonstrate how far away we still were from developing a practical man-carrying powered flying machine. (NASM)

23–25 Although the old professor never lived to see it, the Langley machine did ultimately fly, if only in a greatly altered form. In 1914, aviation pioneer Glenn Curtiss was in the middle of a vicious legal battle with the Wright brothers, who claimed that he had infringed on their patent. In an effort to prove that Langley had discovered the formula for powered flight before the Wrights, Curtiss borrowed the *Aerodrome* from the Smithsonian, made it suitable for taking off from the water, and added numerous other modifications. On May 28, 1914, over Keuka Lake, New York, Professor Langley's *Aerodrome* at last took to the air, as seen in these photos. But of course Curtiss's modifications were substantial and this event was no proof that the *Aerodrome* would have been capable of flying in its original form. (CAM)

26

26   No two individuals are more prominent in the history of aviation than Wilbur and Orville Wright (Orville is at the left in the photo). Wilbur, born in Indiana in 1867, and Orville, born in Ohio in 1871, were the sons of a minister (later bishop) of the United Brethren Church. Both boys showed a great mechanical inclination from an early age and chose to develop those skills rather than attend college. They began with the development of a printing business in their hometown of Dayton, Ohio; then, in 1892 they opened a bicycle shop. In 1896 they began manufacturing their own brand of bicycles. Always avid readers, they were inspired by what they read of Lilienthal's experiments to attempt their own solution to the problem of heavier-than-air flight. After both extensive reading and, in 1899, experimentation with kites, the Wrights were ready to begin work on a full-size, man-carrying glider. On September 12, 1900, Wilbur reached Kitty Hawk, North Carolina, a site that they had discovered would be ideal for experimentation with flying machines. There, he began to assemble their first glider from parts, and Orville joined him on September 28. (NASM)

27   In July 1901 the Wrights returned to Kitty Hawk with a new glider incorporating a better wing shape and control system. Here it is seen being launched from the Kill Devil Hill. This glider made dozens of flights of up to 400 feet. Although it flew well under certain conditions, the Wrights had difficulty in lifting off, turning and maintaining stability. They were encouraged in their experiments by Octave Chanute, who visited them in North Carolina. (NASM)

28   In late 1901 and early 1902 they carried on experiments at their bicycle shop using a wind tunnel of their own design. This enabled them to return to the Kill Devil Hills in late summer of 1902 with a greatly improved glider that could be controlled much more easily. On October 23 they accomplished a flight of over 622 feet. In this photo Wilbur guides the glider over the sands of the Kill Devil Hills. A new movable rudder in the rear (before modification in that month there had been two fixed vanes) provided improved means of control in turns. When they broke camp in late October the Wrights knew they had solved major problems in wing shape, stability and control. (NASM)

29   When the Wrights returned to Kitty Hawk in September 1903, they brought with them the parts to assemble a new, powered flying machine, an enlarged, improved version of their glider. The 152-pound, 8- to 12-hp engine, the propellers and the launching mechanism all had to be of their own design, as they found that no previous designs would suit their purposes. The propellers had been very carefully formed on the basis of their own calculations of aerodynamic characteristics derived from their wind-tunnel experiments. Solving numerous problems at their camp near Kitty Hawk took almost three months, and it was not until December 14, not long before the onset of the harsh Outer Banks winter, that they made their first attempt at powered flight, a failure. Three days later, the Wrights were ready to try again. Finally, at about 10:35 A.M., with Orville at the controls and the engine running smoothly, the Wright "Flyer" lumbered along the rail into a 27-mph wind. After about 40 feet the craft lifted off (at about eight mph) and rose to an altitude of ten feet. It flew on for another 120 feet before landing smoothly. The world's first sustained, controlled powered flight had been achieved. Remarkably, a photo (the one shown here) had been taken to prove it. (NASM)

27

28

29

30 Here the Flyer (dimly visible at the horizon) rests on the desolate sands near Kitty Hawk after the last of the four historic flights made on December 17. On the final one, Wilbur had covered 852 feet and stayed aloft for 59 seconds. A gust of wind that flipped over and damaged the Flyer kept them from flying again for several days. (NASM)

31 The day of their triumph the Wrights sent this telegram to their father, asking him to "inform Press." The press's reaction, however, was that of either disbelief or lack of interest. Nevertheless, the Wright brothers knew that the age of the flying machine had come at last. (CAM)

32 After their success at Kitty Hawk, the Wrights, working now at the "Huffman Prairie," a pasture about eight miles east of Dayton, devoted their efforts to building a more practical version of their airplane. The "Flyer II," completed in 1904, executed the first complete circle ever made by a flying machine; its longest flight was about three miles. Most important, in developing it, the Wrights gained valuable experience. With the "Flyer III" (seen in this photograph), which took to the air in June 1905, they finally had a truly practical machine, able to turn and land with ease. On October 5, it flew for an incredible 39½ minutes and covered over 24 miles. Unbelievably, it would take almost three more years before the skeptical world would accept the accomplishments of these two self-educated geniuses from Ohio. (NASM)

33 The Wrights did no flying in 1906 and 1907. Instead they directed their attention to the practical uses that could be found for their invention. They had offered to sell their machine to the U.S. government as early as January 1905, but at first the government showed no interest. Finally, on February 8, 1908, the War Department offered them a contract requiring that their invention be successfully demonstrated before it would be purchased. The Wrights revamped their 1905 machine to allow the carrying of a passenger. Also, for the first time, the pilot, as well as the passenger, could sit upright instead of lying prone as he had in all previous versions. On August 20, 1908, Orville brought this new plane to Fort Myer, Virginia, to demonstrate it to the U.S. Signal Corps. In this photo the Flyer is being hauled on a supply wagon to the takeoff point. (CAM)

30

Form No. 168.

THE WESTERN UNION TELEGRAPH COMPANY.
INCORPORATED
23,000 OFFICES IN AMERICA.   CABLE SERVICE TO ALL THE WORLD.

This Company **TRANSMITS** and **DELIVERS** messages only o . conditions limiting its liability, which have been assented to by the sender of the following message. Errors can be guarded against only by repeating a message back to the sending station for comparison, and the Company will not hold itself liable for errors or delays in transmission or delivery of **Unrepeated Messages**, beyond the amount of tolls paid thereon, nor in any case where the claim is not presented in writing within sixty days after the message is filed with the Company for transmission.
This is an **UNREPEATED MESSAGE**, and is delivered by request of the sender, under the conditions named above.
ROBERT C. CLOWRY, President and General Manager.

RECEIVED at   170

176 C KA CS 33 Paid.   Via Norfolk Va

Kitty Hawk N C Dec 17

Bishop M Wright

          7 Hawthorne St

Success four flights thursday morning all against twenty one mile

wind started from Level with engine power alone average speed

through air thirty one miles longest 57 seconds inform Press

home ~~their~~ Christmas .   Orevelle Wright   525P

31

32

33

34 Two views of the Wrights' airplane at Fort Myer. (NASM)

35 Flying tests began on September 3, 1908; they were immensely successful from the start. Military officials and visitors were amazed at the ease with which the Wrights flew and how well they controlled their craft. As the testing field at Fort Myer was small, they launched the plane by means of a catapult with a falling weight, a method they had developed at the Huffman Prairie. Here the Flyer soars over a military man on horseback, a contrast of the old and the new. (NASM)

35

36 On September 17, disaster struck. While Orville was flying with Lt. Thomas Selfridge as passenger, a propeller broke and severed a control wire. Immediately the plane plunged to the ground. Orville escaped with his life, though he was seriously injured. Selfridge, however, who had himself been a notable aeronautical experimenter, became the first person to die in an airplane crash. The trials at Fort Myer had to be suspended, but the Wrights did not give up. (NASM)

36

37 On August 8, 1908, around the time that Orville was preparing to demonstrate the Wrights' invention to the Signal Corps, Wilbur took to the air at the Hunaudières racecourse near Le Mans, France, to fulfill a contract with a group of French businessmen. Thus began the Wrights' first public demonstrations in Europe, which sent shock waves through the European aviation community, whose machines had just barely been able to leave the ground. "We are as children compared with the Wrights," said one French would-be aviator. This photo, taken the following year at Pau, France, shows Wilbur aloft with his pupil Paul Tissandier. (NASM)

37

38 In June 1909 Orville returned to Fort Myer with a new, improved machine to complete the demonstrations required by the Wrights' contract with the government. Orville's flights there were witnessed by a number of dignitaries, including President William Howard Taft. The tests were judged to be highly successful and, on August 2, the Wright brothers' aircraft was formally purchased by the U.S. government for $25,000. The Wrights had finally convinced the government of the worth of their revolutionary invention! (CAM)

38

39

39 Information about the results of the Wrights' work with gliders had been released by Octave Chanute in France in 1901, 1902 and 1903, sparking renewed interest in flying. Once the Wrights had built a successful powered machine, however, information available in Europe became less complete, and experimenters had to fend for themselves. Although they lagged far behind the Wrights, many Europeans, especially in France, managed to come up with ingenious designs with elements of their own invention. In 1905 Ernest Archdeacon and Gabriel Voisin designed this glider with pontoons for taking off from the water. It became airborne by being towed behind a boat on the Seine. The glider was constructed by Voisin, who soon formed a company with his brother Charles—the first company created solely for the purpose of building aircraft. In a short time "Voisin Frères" became the premier name in French aircraft manufacturing, and the Voisins' box-kite-like planes could be seen everywhere. Archdeacon, on his part, formed an "aviation syndicate" in an attempt to catch up with the Wrights. (NASM)

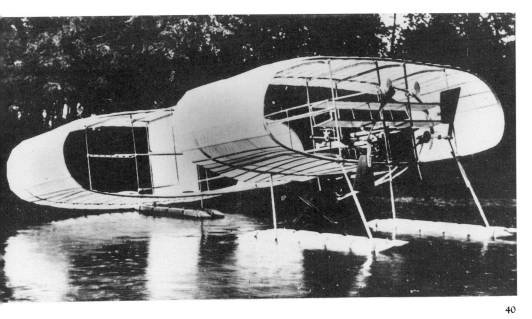

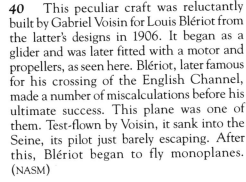

40   This peculiar craft was reluctantly built by Gabriel Voisin for Louis Blériot from the latter's designs in 1906. It began as a glider and was later fitted with a motor and propellers, as seen here. Blériot, later famous for his crossing of the English Channel, made a number of miscalculations before his ultimate success. This plane was one of them. Test-flown by Voisin, it sank into the Seine, its pilot just barely escaping. After this, Blériot began to fly monoplanes. (NASM)

40

41   Jacob C. H. Ellehammer (1871–1946) was a Danish inventor who, in relative obscurity, designed a number of airplanes between 1905 and 1908. On September 12, 1906, he made a powered flight—though tethered to a pole—of 137 feet on the island of Lindholm in this plane, the "Ellehammer II." This was more than a month *before* the first public airplane flight in Europe. Ellehammer's work was notable in that he does not seem to have relied on the designs of any of his predecessors. He failed, however, to develop a workable control system, which had been essential to the success of the Wright brothers. Lack of funds finally forced Ellehammer to abandon his experiments. (NASM)

41

42   Although the strange-looking plane in this photo, the "Vuia I," was a relative failure (it flew for 79 feet in 1906, also before the first public flight), it is notable for being the first monoplane with a tractor propeller. Designed and built by Romanian-born Parisian Trajan Vuia, this aircraft had a rudder but no elevator or ailerons. (NASM)

42

43

44

45

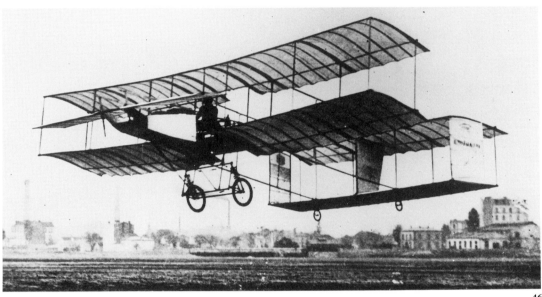

46

43   The first officially recognized flight of a power machine in Europe took place almost three years after the Wrights' success. Brazilian-born Parisian Alberto Santos-Dumont was already known for having successfully flown a number of dirigibles. Then he took to building airplanes. His first plane, shown here, was a canard-type ("tail-first") biplane named the *14 bis*. The box-kite-like forward extension functioned as an elevator. There was no true rudder but Santos-Dumont installed primitive ailerons in the wings. On October 23, 1906, the *14 bis* made the first publicly recorded flight in Europe, a hop of 197 feet, for which Santos-Dumont won the Archdeacon Prize of 3,000 francs for the first European flight of 25 meters or more. On November 12, Santos-Dumont topped this record with a flight of 722 feet. Although the plane's design and performance were less than outstanding, these flights did much to stimulate the development of aviation in Europe. (NASM)

44   Another pioneer inspired by Otto Lilienthal was French artillery captain Louis Ferdinand Ferber (born in 1862). When Octave Chanute provided French aeronautical experimenters with details of the Wright brothers' gliding experiments, Ferber was inspired to work full-time on his own glider. He obtained a leave of absence from the army and by 1903 had progressed to motor-driven machines. In 1906 and 1907, though as yet unsuccessful himself, he prodded the French Ministry of War to negotiate for the purchase of a Wright aircraft. Finally, at Issy-les-Moulineaux near Paris, on July 25, 1908, Ferber, flying a tractor biplane of his own design, rose in brief flight. Until his untimely death fourteen months later, Ferber remained a tireless promoter of the potential of aviation. (NASM)

45   The sculptor Léon Delagrange became interested in flying and ordered one of the Voisin brothers' first planes, shown here. This biplane was first tested at Bagatelle by Charles Voisin, on March 15, 1907. The following month Delagrange flew it for 1640 feet in 40 seconds. This flight would have seemed more of an accomplishment had the aircraft not been totally destroyed when it crashed upon landing! (NASM)

46   Much of the fame of the aircraft of the Voisin brothers was due to the triumphs of Henri Farman. Farman, born in Paris of English parents in 1874, switched his interest from automobile racing to powered flight in 1907 and soon leaped ahead of other European pioneers. In the Voisin biplane shown here, Farman became the third person (after the Wright brothers themselves) to remain in the air for a whole minute. This was at Issy, where he covered 3,379 feet before landing. (NASM)

47

48

49

47 The fourth Voisin plane was also sold to Henri Farman. This time he made modifications of his own to the elevator, tail and wing dihedral. Powered by a 50-hp engine, this plane proved itself airworthy by making twenty short flights at Issy between September 30 and November 30, 1907. It was on January 13 of the following year, however, that Farman really distinguished himself in this plane when he flew a complete circle of about a mile, for which he was awarded the 50,000-franc Deutsch-Archdeacon Prize for the first flight of a kilometer or more in a closed circuit. (NASM)

48 One of the most influential pioneers of early flight was Glenn H. Curtiss of Hammondsport, New York. Born in 1878, Curtiss, like the Wrights, started off in the bicycle business, which led to a career in the manufacture of the earliest American motorcycles. Curtiss built his own engines, known for their power relative to their small size. He became involved with heavier-than-air flight in 1907, when his reputation as a skillful builder of engines, which had begun to be used in airships as well, brought him to the attention of Alexander Graham Bell. The inventor of the telephone had become interested in the mechanics of flight and, with his wife, had formed the Aerial Experiment Association (AEA) in Nova Scotia. There were four flying members, including Curtiss, who also became the director of experiments and built all the machines in Hammondsport. Professor Bell provided fatherly guidance and expert advice, Mrs. Bell encouragement and money. This 1907 photo shows the group's first project, a glider, their first experience with flying. (NASM)

49 The first powered aircraft built by the AEA was called the *Red Wing,* after the color of its silk-fabric surfaces. It was designed by Thomas Selfridge, a U.S. Army lieutenant who had joined the Bells' group with the permission of President Roosevelt. Built in seven weeks at Hammondsport, the *Red Wing,* powered by a 40-hp Curtiss V-8 engine, was tested on March 12, 1908, on frozen Keuka Lake nearby. Piloted by Casey Baldwin, another member of the AEA, the first short flight of 319 feet resulted in a crash. Five days later the *Red Wing* made one more brief flight just before which this photo was taken. (NASM)

50 After the flight of the *Red Wing,* on March 17, 1908—its last, for after flying 120 feet the craft was wrecked beyond all repair, as seen here. (NASM)

50

51

51–53   Following this initial limited success, the AEA immediately began their second machine. This new craft, designed by Baldwin and named the *White Wing*, was completed on May 9, 1908. Built along the same lines as the *Red Wing*, the most obvious change was the addition of a wheeled undercarriage. Tested on Stony Brook Farm near Hammondsport, where these three photos were taken, the *White Wing* first flew on May 18, for a distance of about 300 feet. It made five flights in all, the longest of which was 1200 feet on May 21. This plane, like its predecessor, was badly damaged on this last flight, and once more the group immediately began work on another aircraft, this time with Glenn Curtiss as the principal designer. (CAM)

54   Alexander Graham Bell (center) confers with Casey Baldwin, the designer of the *White Wing*, before its May 18 flight. (NASM)

55   Curtiss riding a tricycle device, on June 19, 1908, used to test the hinged wingtips that served as ailerons in the AEA's next plane, the *June Bug*. (CAM)

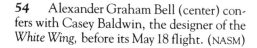

52

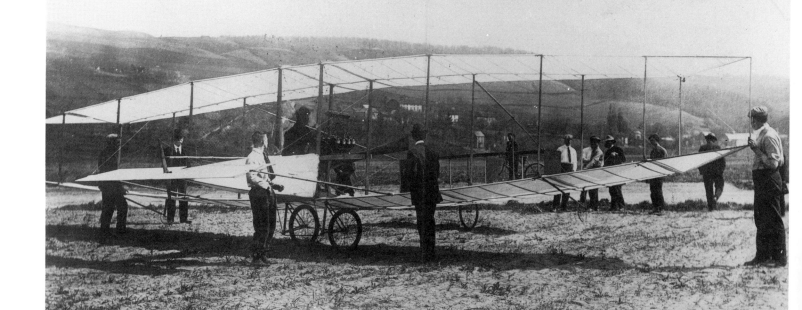

53

54

56

57

58

59

60

56–59 The *June Bug,* so named because it was built and flown in June, was one of the AEA's most successful aircraft. It had a forward elevator and a rear rudder as well as a form of ailerons. First flown on June 21, 1908, this plane's most notable accomplishment was the winning of the *Scientific American* trophy on July 4 for the first American flight to exceed one kilometer. The *June Bug* easily captured the prize with a flight of about a mile. This was one of the first highly publicized flights in America. In all, the *June Bug* made a total of 18 flights in a three-week period, during which time these four photos were taken. (CAM)

60 In the fall of 1908 the *June Bug* was fitted with twin floats and renamed the *Loon.* Several attempts were made in November to fly this hydroaeroplane from the surface of Keuka Lake, but without success. With our more sophisticated knowledge of hydrodynamics, we now know that this experiment was doomed to failure, for the flat-bottomed floats created a suction that was impossible to overcome when the engine—weak to begin with—tried to pull the craft off the water's surface. The AEA then decided to begin yet another plane, and no more time was wasted on the *June Bug/Loon.* (CAM)

61

62

61 The next plane constructed by the AEA, the *Silver Dart*, was in some ways their most important. Powered by a 50-hp engine, the *Silver Dart* was larger than the *June Bug* and had a more refined airfoil. After completion at Curtiss' Hammondsport manufacturing facility, the plane was test-flown nearby on December 12, 1908. Then, in early 1909, the aircraft was taken to Baddeck, Nova Scotia, then the home of Bell and his family, where it was flown successfully by J. A. D. McCurdy on February 23 (as seen here). This was notable as the first flight of an airplane in Canada. The next day, the *Silver Dart* made a flight of 4½ miles, including several turns. (NASM)

62 A closeup of McCurdy in the *Silver Dart* on the ice at Baddeck in February 1909. Note the low-mounted engine, the chain drive to the propeller, and the radiator—the strange-looking vertical tubing behind McCurdy. (CAM)

63 Professor Bell had always been a believer in the superiority of a tetrahedral-cell wing design. After this design had been used in kites, the *Cygnet II*, a powered plane with this wing conformation, was built by the AEA and tested twice at Baddeck. To Bell's bitter disappointment, it was a total failure. Here McCurdy is seen at the wheel on February 22, 1909, the day before he became the first man to fly an airplane in Canada. (CAM)

64 In the spring of 1909 the Aerial Experiment Association was dissolved. Glenn Curtiss returned to Hammondsport to start his own airplane-manufacturing company in partnership with Augustus Herring. McCurdy, in deference to Bell, returned to experiment with tetrahedral-cell aircraft in 1912. Between March 1 and March 17 of that year, several tests of the *Cygnet III* (shown here with McCurdy at the controls), a greatly modified version of the *Cygnet II*, were made at Baddeck. In one attempt, the *Cygnet III* just barely flew. Thus, to a limited degree, Bell's ideas were finally borne out. (NASM)

63

64

EUROPEAN AVIATORS
AND THEIR MACHINES

65

65 To build a flying machine that could take off vertically was the focus of inventive French mechanic Paul Cornu. After overcoming numerous difficulties, Cornu finally built a machine powered by a 24-hp Antoinette engine and mounted on four bicycle wheels. The motor drove twin 20-foot-long propellers supported on outriggers. At the end of 1907, Cornu ascended in this machine to a height of five feet and remained there for one minute. This proto-helicopter was the first flying machine to have risen from the ground using rotor blades instead of wings. Cornu is seen here seated at the controls of his machine. (NASM)

66

66 The chief pilot for the French Wright Company in the 1909–10 period was Eugène Lefebvre, whose aerial antics earned him the distinction of being the first stunt pilot. At the first international aviation tournament in Rheims, France, in 1909, Lefebvre placed second in the speed contest. He also performed primitive acrobatics there in the Wright Model A in which he is seen in this photo. On July 18 of that year he became the first man to fly an airplane in Holland. On September 7, Lefebvre became the first European to be killed in a plane crash. (NASM)

67 One of the most dashing aviators of the pre-World War I period was Claude Grahame-White of England. A wealthy aristocrat turned auto racer, Grahame-White was soon drawn to aviation. He attended the tournament at Rheims and there he purchased a Blériot. By the following year he had opened his own flying school in France. In April 1910 he returned to his native England to compete for the *Daily Mail* prize of £10,000 for making the first flight between London and Manchester (185 miles). Grahame-White lost the race to Frenchman Louis Paulhan but while competing he became the first person to fly an airplane at night. In September he went to the United States to compete at the Harvard-Boston air meet (where he is seen in this photograph). There, flying his speedy Blériot, he won in virtually every category. During the meet, wealthy society beauties paid $500 for rides with him. (NASM)

67

68

69

68 In October 1910 Grahame-White won the Gordon Bennett speed race at the aviation meet at Belmont Park, New York. Later that month he flew to Washington, D.C., and landed on a street next to the White House. Many distinguished Washingtonians gathered to see him take off later that day, an event captured in this photograph. (NASM)

69 Another French inventor who worked with early helicopter designs was Louis Breguet (seen here in a closeup portrait), who as early as 1906 built a "gyroplane" combining the fixed wing surfaces of an airplane with the revolving blades of a helicopter. On July 22, 1908, Breguet is said to have negotiated a distance of 65 feet in this machine. After minimal success with helicopters, Breguet turned to conventional aircraft. His "Breguet IV" set a world record when it carried six persons in August 1910. Breguet continued to develop his machines, and one of them became a favorite of the French army in World War I. (NASM)

70 On November 29, 1906, Austrian designer Igo Etrich (seen here with his son) made the first brief airplane hop in Vienna. Etrich's "Taube" ("Dove"), designed in 1910, was a graceful, birdlike monoplane that used a novel wing-warping system of control. The design proved so efficient that in 1911 production rights were sold to Rumpler and eventually ten different firms in Germany were building Taubes. Early in World War I, the aircraft was used for reconnaissance. (NASM)

71 Beginning on May 28, 1911, an air race was held between Paris and Rome, attracting the greatest aviators in Europe. Over the course of the race, the machines were pushed to their limits, as every minute counted in the scoring. The race was ultimately won by Jean Conneau. Of the 21 aviators entered, only four finished the race. One of these was René Vidart, seen here in his new streamlined, fast Deperdussin—the first public appearance of a monoplane that would eventually make aviation history. (NASM)

70

71

72

73

72 Having first flown at age 47, Samuel Franklin Cody was the oldest of the pioneering aviators. Previously a Texas cowboy, Wild West showman and gold prospector, Cody, even after he had moved permanently to England (he became a naturalized British subject), typically wore a ten-gallon hat and cowboy boots and carried a Colt revolver. Shortly after the turn of the century, when he was already living in England, he built and flew huge man-carrying kites that demonstrated the potential of the military use of aircraft. His first plane, British Army Aeroplane No. 1, was the first aircraft to fly in England, on October 16, 1908. In 1910 he built a new machine of improved design (shown here), and with it won the Michelin Cup race on December 31, covering 185.5 miles in four hours 47 minutes. (NASM)

73 Cody's planes were of large, clumsy design, yet they proved to be an enormous stimulus to aviation in England. Although he could not read or write, Cody had a flair for both aviation and publicity, as seen in this photo of a flight with several passengers. (NASM)

74 Igor Sikorsky, a leading aviation pioneer, was born in Kiev, Russia, in 1889. He attended the Naval Academy in St. Petersburg and then the Polytechnic Institute of Kiev, where he studied engineering. Having dreamt of flying machines from an early age, Sikorsky first became interested in aviation in a practical way when he read a newspaper account of a Wright brothers flight in 1908. He traveled to France in 1909, where he met many of the early aviators and studied flying with Captain Ferdinand Ferber. A

tinkerer from his youth, Sikorsky set out to build his own planes. For some time, during which he built four airplanes and two early attempts at a helicopter, his efforts met with no success. On May 17, 1911, he finally had a successful flight in his model S-5. Then he began work on the S-6. This had disappointing performance characteristics at first, but the young, ambitious aircraft designer was stimulated to engage in further research. The refined version, the S-6-A, completed at the end of 1911, was a resounding success, and earned Sikorsky a prize as well as recognition as a major designer of aircraft. The S-6-A, seen here, could carry two passengers in addition to the pilot and set a speed record for a plane of this configuration when it was clocked at over seventy mph. (NASM)

75 After working on two other small planes, Sikorsky embarked on one of the most ambitious projects anyone had yet undertaken: an enormous aircraft with multiple engines. Named *Le Grand* (and later, officially, *Russian Knight*), this plane, shown here, was the largest anyone had constructed to date, as well as the first to have four propellers. Weighing four and a half tons and powered by four 100-hp Argus engines, it had dual controls, a fully enclosed cabin with large windows, and an open observation platform. It first flew on May 13, 1913. Sikorsky soon modified it to improve its flying characteristics. Altogether it made 53 successful flights; on one, it carried seven passengers and stayed aloft nearly two full hours, a new record. Late in 1913 it was severely damaged in a freak accident, when the engine of another aircraft flying overhead fell out and smashed a wing. Successors of *Le Grand* were used as bombers in World War I. (CAM)

76 Dutch pilot and aircraft designer Anthony Fokker was also inspired by the Wrights' visit to France in 1908. In 1911, he built his first aircraft, a monoplane type named "Die Spinne" ("The Spider"). Then he built two, more refined, versions, with which he made many successful exhibition flights. He was encouraged by his success to open his own factory in Germany in 1912. Fokker Spinnes were widely used in both civilian and military flying schools in Germany before World War I. Then, Fokker went on to become one of the great producers of combat aircraft for the war. (NASM)

77 The sleek monoplane designed for Armand Deperdussin in 1912 by the brilliant engineer Louis Béchereau represents one of the great advances in aircraft design. It had a "monocoque" (molded plywood) fuselage and a large propeller spinner. This streamlining—together with two seven-cylinder rotary engines—helped it break records and win contests. The first version of this plane won the Gordon Bennett cup in Chicago on September 9, 1912, with a speed of 108 mph. Mounted on floats and fitted with a more powerful engine, the Deperdussin won the first race for seaplanes, in Monaco, in 1913. Finally, at Rheims, on September 29, it won the Schneider trophy and became the first airplane to fly faster than 200 kilometers (124 miles) an hour. Maurice Prévost, the pilot of this remarkable aircraft, is seen here in its cockpit. (NASM)

75

76

77

78

78 This unique aircraft designed and built by Romanian-born Frenchman Henri Coanda is often considered the forerunner of the modern jet. Through a series of gears, the plane's piston engine drove a centrifugal blower mounted in the forward part of the fuselage. This was really the first "ducted fan" aircraft. It was also ahead of its time in that it was streamlined, with a minimum of struts and wires. Coanda's plane would be remembered today as a truly revolutionary machine, if not for one detail: it never got off the ground, primarily because of its weak power plant. (NASM)

79, 80 Alberto Santos-Dumont, the man who had made the first publicly recorded flight in Europe, also developed the world's first practical light plane, the "Demoiselle" ("Damselfly"). A prototype first flew in November 1907; the production version debuted in March 1909. Although not as powerful or fast as other aircraft, the Demoiselle was cheap and simple. Powered by a two-cylinder engine (at first 28 hp, then improved to 35 hp), the little craft featured a bamboo-tubing fuselage. The pilot sat under the wing. (**Photo 79** shows Santos-Dumont himself in the pilot's seat; **photo 80** shows a later version with another pilot.) The Demoiselle was sold in numbers in the 1909–19 period, and became especially popular after having been exhibited at the Grand Palais in Paris in 1910. By this time its creator, who had become seriously ill, had begun to withdraw from aviation. Finally, depressed, it is said, by the destructive uses to which aircraft were being put, Santos-Dumont took his life in 1932. (NASM)

79

80

81

82

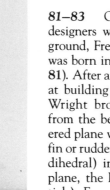

81–83 One of only a few early aircraft designers with a sound engineering background, Frenchman Robert Esnault-Pelterie was born in 1881 (shown close-up in **photo 81**). After an unsuccessful attempt, in 1904, at building a glider in the manner of the Wright brothers, he altogether departed from the beaten path and designed a powered plane with a short fuselage, no vertical fin or rudder and a slight anhedral (negative dihedral) in the wings. With this unusual plane, the REP-1 (REP being his own initials), Esnault-Pelterie managed to fly just under 2,000 feet in November 1907. His next model, the REP-2 (**photo 82**), was considerably more refined, with a large fin and rudder, but it was still basically unstable. Nevertheless it managed a number of flights in the spring and summer of 1909, the best being one of five miles. Esnault-Pelterie finally achieved success with a more conventional design, the Type "D" (**photo 83**) which, carrying pilot and passenger, set a speed record in December 1910. REP monoplanes were used by the air services of several countries in the years before World War I. Soon Esnault-Pelterie shifted his attention to research in rocket propulsion and stopped designing airplanes. (NASM)

83

M. NIEUPORT

1290. – Monoplan Nieuport

Surface portante 14 mq, envergure 8 m., largeur des ailes 2 m., longueur de l'appareil 7 m. Poids en ordre de marche 285 kgr. Stabilisateur automatique; le châssis monté sur roues et patins, gouvernail de profondeur monoplan, gouvernail de direction biplan, levier unique de commande, commandant les 2 gouvernails. Moteur Anzani 20 HP à l'avant actionnant hélice Chauvière de 2. 40 de diamètre et 1. 50 de pas, et tournant à 1290 tours.

J. H.

84

84   Edouard de Nieuport (born Edouard de Niéport in 1875) was originally a motorcycle racer, later a manufacturer of electrical devices. In 1908 he took up aviation at Issy, where he built his first aircraft, a small monoplane powered by a 20-hp engine. After successfully flying this aircraft in 1909, in 1910 he developed a more refined monoplane with a fully enclosed fuselage and powered by a 50-hp Gnôme engine. Nieuport's planes, having less wing camber (front-to-back curvature) than other planes, were faster, and they began to set new records and soon became synonymous with speed. Nieuport himself was killed in a plane crash in 1911 and his brother Charles, his partner, died similarly in 1913. The company, however, went on to build some of the greatest fighters of World War I. (NASM)

85   The British and Colonial Aeroplane Company (better known as Bristol Aircraft, its name later on) was formed in February 1910 by Sir George White, Chairman of the Bristol Tramway Company. Bristol's first successful aircraft, two-seat copies of the Farman biplane, became known as the Bristol "Boxkite" (seen here). Powered by a 50-hp Gnôme engine, the Boxkite was first flown on July 29, 1910. This plane was a great commercial success, remaining in production until 1914. In all, 130 were built, many for export. Some of these were for the British Army and the Bristol Flying school at Brooklands. (NASM)

85

86   A Deperdussin monoplane of the 1910–11 period. This speedy aircraft, powered by a 50-hp Clerget engine, featured an unusual six-blade propeller. Doubtless this experiment was not successful, as such planes were not seen again. Nevertheless, it was typical of the unusual designs that were being tried out all the time in the pre-World War I period, when aeronautical science still had so much to learn. (CAM)

87   Adolphe Pégoud, born in France in 1899, went from an interest in mechanical things to an interest in aviation. In 1913 he joined the Blériot staff. He made history in that year when he became the first pilot to jump from an airplane in flight, deliberately leaping from an old Blériot during a stunt flight and floating down by parachute. In the same year, on September 2, Pégoud astounded crowds at Juvisy aerodrome by flying his airplane upside down. He topped this on September 21 when, in a specially reinforced Blériot, he "looped the loop." (This is often considered to have been the first loop ever flown; this feat, however, had actually been performed twelve days earlier by the Russian officer Lt. Peter Nikolaievich Nesterov at Kiev.) Pégoud then performed his loop many times over on a highly successful tour. The stunt was quickly copied by aviators around the world. (CAM)

86

87

88

88 British army Lt. John W. Dunne (1875–1949) was appointed kite designer at Farnborough, England, in 1905, and immediately concerned himself with developing an inherently stable aircraft. He devised a machine with two constant-chord (width) swept-back wings in the form of an arrowhead, with no tail or fuselage. In essence this was the world's first pair of "flying wings." Although ahead of its time conceptually, unfortunately this aircraft did not perform well. Dunne's first moderately successful and first real powered aircraft was his D.4, first flown in 1908. In 1912 he built the machine in this photo, the D.8, the last and most successful of his aircraft. Here a single pusher propeller replaced the chain-driven pair used on earlier models. The aircraft also had ailerons at all four wing tips. It was first flown in June 1912. (NASM)

89 Hubert Latham, born in Paris to English parents in 1883, was a bachelor sportsman equally at home in French and English society. He took a degree from Oxford and was involved in speedboat racing. In 1909 airplane builder Léon Levavasseur asked Latham to be his chief pilot; Latham immediately accepted, as he saw aviation to be an exciting new sport. He soon became known as "the gentleman of the air." In the 1909–11 period the dashing Latham became closely identified with his beautiful Antoinette aircraft. (NASM)

89

90, 91 "Antoinette" airplanes were certainly among the most famous and perhaps the most beautiful aircraft of the pre-World War I period. Named for Antoinette Gastambide, the daughter of the company director, these planes were designed by the brilliant engineer Léon Levavasseur. Antoinettes were powered by eight-cylinder Antoinette engines ranging from 24 to 100 hp; these engines were also used in many other early French aircraft. From the moment it appeared, the Antoinette was considered a very elegant, aerodynamically advanced design. It featured a long, slim fuselage, trapezoidal wings and a cruciform tail. The Antoinette IV first flew in October 1908 and was modified and improved in early 1909. It had ailerons, but these worked poorly. In the type VI and later models, wing warping was used instead for turning, as in the original Wright Flyer. On June 5, 1909, Latham set a world record for monoplanes, staying aloft in his Antoinette for one hour, seven minutes. On June 12, he flew forty kilometers in 39 minutes before a group of parliamentary officials. **Photo 90** dates from the October 1910 international air tournament at Belmont Park, New York, **photo 91** from January 1911. (NASM)

90

92, 93 Latham also made two unsuccessful attempts to cross the English Channel in his Antoinette. The first was on July 19, 1909 (**photo 92**), just a few days before Blériot's successful crossing. Latham took off from Calais, and things seemed to go well until, after seven miles, the engine of his Antoinette failed and he was forced down at sea. Both the plane and pilot were rescued by the crew of a French destroyer that had been tracking his attempted crossing (**photo 93**). Latham made a second try on July 27 (Blériot had already crossed but Latham had wagered that he would cross the Channel himself before August). This time his plane's engine failed when he was only a mile from the British shore. Latham was knocked unconscious and the plane destroyed, but the intrepid aviator recovered quickly enough to participate in the Rheims aviation meet at the end of August, flying a new Antoinette. There he took second place in the distance race and first place in the altitude contest, having climbed to 509 feet. (NASM)

92

93

94

95

96

94   At the Antoinette flying school in 1910. In this primitive form of ground instruction, the barrel would be tilted and the student would have to use the controls to right it. (CAM)

95   Henri Farman in his first Voisin plane, late in 1907. With this aircraft Farman won the Archdeacon prize on November 9 with a flight of some 3380 feet. This was also the first flight of more than a minute in duration to be made in a non-Wright aircraft. (NASM)

96   Farman in the Voisin biplane in which he won the Deutsch-Archdeacon Prize for the first flight of over a kilometer, on January 13, 1908. This aircraft had a wingspan of approximately 33 feet and was powered by a 50-hp Antoinette engine. (NASM)

97   The Voisin biplane on display in 1909 at the first French Salon d'Aviation. (NASM)

98   In November 1908 Farman attempted to convert his Voisin biplane into a triplane, seen in this photo. In October he had added ailerons, the first really practical ailerons to be seen on a European plane. This modification was successful, but the triplane configuration was not, and performance suffered. In 1909 Farman sold this machine to an Austrian. (NASM)

99   Henri Rougier, a champion cyclist and race-car driver, learned to fly in a Voisin plane just before the 1909 Rheims tournament. Thereafter he won his share of prizes at other aviation meets. Here he pilots his Voisin over the water at Monaco in 1909. (CAM)

97

98

99

100

101

100, 101   After the failure of the Farman-modified Voisin triplane, Farman ordered a new plane from the Voisin brothers. To his astonishment they manufactured the plane and then sold it to someone else! Farman immediately set about building his own aircraft, the "Henry Farman" (born in France to English parents, for years Farman used the English spelling of his first name). The Henry Farman, with a full set of ailerons and twin rudders, and powered by a 50-hp Gnôme engine, was efficient and reliable, and it proved to be a far better aircraft than its Voisin predecessors. It first flew in April 1909 and at the Rheims meet in August distinguished itself by winning several prizes for its builder and pilot, including first prize for distance, after an outstanding flight of 112 miles. This plane, seen here, immediately became a standard for European aircraft in the pre–World War I period. In fact, in the historic London-Manchester race between Louis Paulhan and Claude Grahame-White in 1910, *both* men flew Henry Farmans! (NASM)

102

102 Roger Sommer in his Henry Farman at the Rheims air meet. Note the wicker seat and the foot controls for the ailerons. Sommer would later become known as a builder of planes along Farmanesque lines. (CAM)

103

103 A Henry Farman on, purportedly, the first aerial hunting trip, showing its ability to carry three people. (CAM)

104 A closeup of the Henry Farman's rotary engine. Note how this engine was mounted behind the propeller. The crankshaft was bolted to the plane. (CAM)

104

105 By all measures Louis Blériot, born in Cambrai, France, in 1872, was one of the outstanding figures of early aviation. After having established a successful automotive business, Blériot was attracted to aviation around the turn of the century. He then had built for him a string of aircraft of various designs. At first his efforts were rewarded with disaster. The Blériot I (1902) was an unsuccessful ornithopter (predecessor of the helicopter). The Blériot II of 1905, a float-mounted biplane built for him by Voisin, was equally unsuccessful. The float plane Blériot III of 1906 also failed to fly, as did a land plane version, the Blériot IV. The Blériot V had a canard design and mounted an Antoinette engine. This model finally made a few short hops at Bagatelle in 1907. The Blériot VI was a tandem-wing tractor monoplane that also made short hops, at Issy in the same year. Toward the end of the year, the Blériot VII, which marked a significant advance and was technologically sophisticated for its time, made many successful flights. The Blériot VIII, featuring the first ailerons on a European plane (Farman fitted his Voisin with ailerons at around this time, with, as it turned out, greater success) flew over 17 miles in October 1908. In December, three Blériot machines were displayed in Paris. Two of them, the IX and X, were failures; with the third, however, the Blériot XI (seen here), which had not yet been flown, a whole new era in aviation was to dawn. (NASM)

105

106 The Blériot XI, which was modified in a number of ways at various times, in one form or another became the classic tractor monoplane of the pre-World War I period. When first flown at Issy on January 23, 1909, it was powered by a 30-hp REP engine driving a crude four-blade metal propeller, as seen here. (CAM)

107 In April 1909 the Blériot XI was fitted with a more efficient propeller and a new 25-hp Anzani engine. Unhappy with the way the ailerons had functioned on his previous planes, Blériot now returned to the system of wing warping introduced by the Wright brothers. The Blériot XI was, in fact, the first European aircraft to employ wing warping effectively. Throughout the spring and summer of 1909 this plane made many excellent flights. (NASM)

106

107

108, 109 In 1908 Lord Northcliffe offered a prize of £1,000 for the first flight across the English Channel. Blériot, now prepared to compete for this prize, took off in his model XI on the rainy morning of July 25, 1909, and, after a labored crossing of about a half hour, landed in a field near Dover Castle. Blériot returned to France a national hero. On a larger scale, the political and military repercussions of his flight were enormous. England, once isolated from the Continent by a substantial body of water, was now linked to it by air. The new ease of access had its positive side, but this also meant that Britain was now open to attack from the air. (NASM)

108

109

110 The Blériot XI, now world famous, was soon in production. At first it was successfully flown by competitive fliers such as Delagrange and Leblanc. Later it was used by the French military right into the first years of World War I. (CAM)

111 A second great flight in a Blériot monoplane was made on September 23, 1910, when Peruvian pilot Georges Chavez made the first airplane flight over the Alps. Competing for a prize of 70,000 lire, Chavez's Blériot had to function at an altitude of some 6,000 feet in order to make the crossing. Flying through cold, turbulent air, Chavez's frail craft made the crossing from Switzerland to Italy in 42 minutes. As he was landing, however, the plane malfunctioned and crashed. Chavez was severely injured and died four days later. (NASM)

110

111

112

113

114

115

112 Throughout the 1910–11 period, many of the greatest aviators in the world flew successors of the Blériot XI. Ultimately, with model XXVII, the plane was given the more powerful 50-hp Gnôme engine, which enabled it to win the Gordon Bennett speed race. The Gnôme was a popular, efficient engine, but as a rotary engine it had a design that is now obsolete. The propeller was bolted directly to the engine and the entire assembly revolved around the crankshaft, which was bolted to the plane. This was a necessary arrangement with these early motors, as the only way to air-cool them was to spin the entire engine! (CAM)

113 V. D. Yoncheere, a Belgian aviator, and his Blériot at the Philadelphia Navy Yard during a demonstration in 1912. Note the fuel tank suspended under the fuselage. (CAM)

114 Even before his successful Channel crossing, Blériot had designed another model aircraft, type XII, a larger monoplane with a high wing, first flown in May 1909. The engine was located below the wing, where the pilot sat also, as with the Demoiselle. As this aircraft originally had poor directional control, it was given a large ventral fin. Blériot's aim had been to produce a plane able to carry more than just one passenger. He realized this goal on June 12, 1909, when his type XII became the first aircraft in the world to carry a pilot and two passengers. A Blériot XII was also the first plane owned by Claude Grahame-White. (CAM)

115 Another interesting design was Blériot's *Aérobus* of 1911. On March 23, 1911, this plane made a three-mile flight with eight passengers, a new world record. During World War I, Blériot was one of the world's largest producers of military training aircraft. (CAM)

116

116 The first woman in the world to fly in an airplane was Thérèse Peltier (right). A French sculptress, she was a friend of Léon Delagrange and happened to be in Turin, Italy, when he was there with his plane on July 8, 1908. When Mlle. Peltier declared her desire to be the first woman to fly, Delagrange obliged by flying her some 650 feet, twelve feet off the ground. (CAM)

117 An unknown English aviatrix, ca. 1912. (CAM)

118, 119 Women also took to the air in the pre-World War I period, but not in great numbers, as most flying schools refused to accept them. Belgium's first woman pilot, later licensed in France, was Hélène Dutrieu, who first flew in April 1909. Five months later she made world headlines by flying from Ostend to Bruges, a distance of 28 miles. During the flight she also reached an altitude of 1300 feet, higher than any woman had yet flown. In May 1911 she competed in a race in Florence, Italy, defeating the 14 male contestants and winning the coveted King's Cup. She also won the women's endurance contest at the Nassau Boulevard meet that fall. In December 1911 she set a new world nonstop-flight record for women, covering 158 miles in 2 hours 58 minutes. Unfortunately, most of the coverage she received in the press related to the fact that she flew without a corset. Flying without a corset, she explained, gave her more freedom of movement. In the early days of aviation, all female pilots had great difficulty devising a flying outfit that was both practical and ladylike in the harsh exposed cockpits. (NASM)

117

118

AMERICAN AVIATORS AND THEIR MACHINES

120 As the 1908 Army trials were cut short by an accident, Orville Wright could not resume his flight tests for the Army at Fort Myer until the end of June 1909. This time both Wilbur and Orville were present. Earlier in 1909 Wilbur had been giving flying demonstrations at Pau, France, where he was visited by many dignitaries, including two kings. While in France, Wilbur taught several Frenchmen to fly and he set up a company for the manufacture of Wright aeroplanes under license. On August 2, after the Wrights had successfully completed their testing, their Flyer was formally purchased by the U.S. government as Army Aeroplane No. 1. Here it is seen flying over the enthralled throngs at Fort Myer. (NASM)

120

121

122

121   After the Army testing, Orville returned to Europe while Wilbur gave a series of spectacular demonstrations in America. On September 29 and October 4, 1909, Wilbur flew several demonstration flights as part of the Hudson–Fulton Celebration in New York. Here, on September 29, he can be seen flying low over Governors Island, his operations base in New York harbor. The long, dark shape under the plane is a sealed canoe that Wilbur hoped would keep the plane afloat if he landed in the water. On October 4, he made a 21-mile round-trip flight to Grant's Tomb in upper Manhattan, one of the most dangerous over-water flights that anyone had yet made. (NASM)

122   At the end of 1909 Orville was in France helping to organize the newly formed French Wright Company. The company produced several successful aircraft. Financial returns were less than expected since the French government refused to buy foreign aircraft. Still, Wright airplanes, interestingly, *were* in production in France while there was no organized company for their manufacture in America. This and the next five photos of the manufacturing operation of the French Wright Company in 1909 show the unique craftsmanship involved in the production of one of these early aircraft. Each part had to be individually hand-carved and fitted. This view shows the framework of the rudders. (CAM)

123

123 Fitting the skids to the lower wing. Note the way each wing rib is built up. (CAM)

124 Assembling the forward elevators. (CAM)

125 The wing struts of the upper wing (seen here inverted). (CAM)

126 The wing spars are being joined and the struts fitted. Wright struts simply slid on a loop and were braced by wires. They were not rigidly attached as in other aircraft. (CAM)

127 The engine and chain-drive assembly of a completed aircraft are being tested. (CAM)

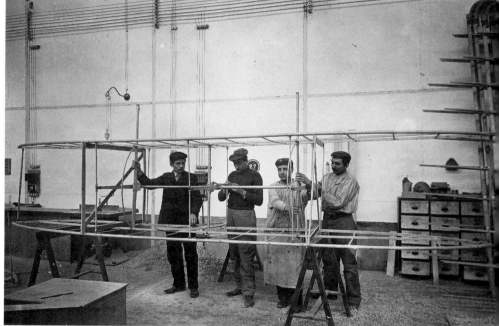

124

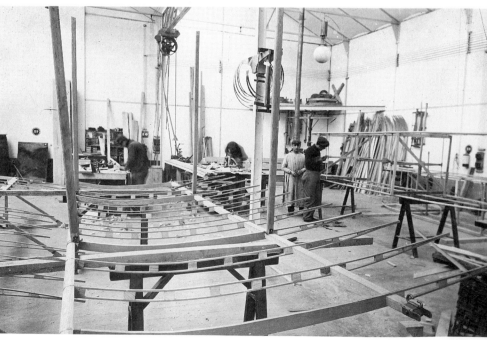

125

126

127

128–131 In April 1909, Wilbur took a Wright aircraft to Rome for a series of demonstration flights. These flights had been arranged by King Victor Emmanuel III of Italy, who was especially interested in the problems of flight. Wilbur also trained two Italians to fly at this time. Between April 15 and 26, Wilbur made more than 50 flights, often carrying a passenger. The flights were witnessed by large and enthusiastic crowds. These four photos were taken at Centocelle Field near Rome sometime during this period. At left in **photo 128** is the derrick the Wrights used to launch their Flyers where limited space was available. The launching rail is clearly visible under the plane. In **photo 130** an Italian pilot is at the controls; note the jury-rigged seat next to him. (CAM)

132 On March 26, 1910, the Wrights opened their first flying school near Montgomery, Alabama, where the climate was suitable for year-round operation. Orville served as instructor, and several of their first students stayed on to work as Wright Company pilots. Here a Wright Model "A" flies over a freshly plowed Alabama field. (CAM)

133 In 1910 the Wrights developed their very successful Model "B" aircraft. Powered by a four-cylinder, 30-hp Wright engine, this was the first Wright plane without forward elevators, instead relying on a more conventional single elevator in the rear. Also, the clumsy skids of previous models were replaced by a four-wheeled landing gear. The Wrights, however, still relied on an awkward chain-drive system. The Model B was an immediate hit, with several being ordered by the U.S. government, and variants developed for racing. Here a Model B soars overhead with pilot and passenger. (CAM)

128

129

130

131

132

134

135

136

134 One of the stars of the Wright brothers' exhibition team was 24-year-old Ralph Johnstone, a former trick cyclist from Kansas City. At the Belmont Park Meet on October 31, 1910, Johnstone set a new world record for altitude—a remarkable 9,712 feet—in his Model B (in which he is seen in this photo). In one of his attempts to break the altitude record, Johnstone flew into the teeth of a stiff wind. His airspeed of 40 mph was no match for the 80-mph winds at altitude, but he managed to get his plane down safely in a clearing 55 miles east of Belmont Park, having been blown backward the entire way. Less than three weeks later, Johnstone was in Denver, putting on a demonstration of tight turns and dives, when the wings of his plane folded up and he was killed. (NASM)

135 Another star of the Wright brothers' team was Arch Hoxsey, age 26. After attending the Los Angeles Air Meet in 1910, Hoxsey, an automobile mechanic and race-car driver, immediately headed to the Wright School in Ohio and stayed on as one of their pilots. At every air meet, he and Ralph Johnstone dueled each other for new altitude and endurance records. (NASM)

136 On October 11, 1910, Hoxsey took former President Theodore Roosevelt for his first airplane ride in St. Louis. Roosevelt thus became the first President to fly. On December 31, 1910, Hoxsey was in Los Angeles while trying to beat his own world altitude record of 11,474 feet. Flying in high winds, Hoxsey failed to recover from a tailspin at 7,000 feet and was killed. (NASM)

137 Bitten by the flying bug, Harry Nelson Atwood, trained at MIT as an electrical engineer, abandoned his business near Boston to enroll in the new Wright Flying School in Ohio. He quickly became a proficient pilot, and within three months of his first flight he made a record-breaking 461-mile flight from Boston to Washington. At Washington he landed on the White House lawn. Then, between August 14 and 25, 1910, he made an even more remarkable 1,256-mile flight from St. Louis to New York (with eleven stops). Atwood, seen here in his Model B, was one of the few early pilots to die of natural causes, in 1967 at age 83. (NASM)

138 George Beatty, seen here standing on a skid of his Model B (note the two seats), at the Brighton Beach Race Track, Brooklyn, 1910. Racetracks were frequently used for aviation exhibitions because of their grassy open spaces and grandstands. (CAM)

137

138

139

140

141

139 Another Wright-trained pilot was Frank Coffyn, who astonished New Yorkers with his Wright hydroaeroplane. With its two pontoons of aluminum, the plane was nicknamed the "flying toboggan." It was flown off both water and ice in New York harbor in the winter of 1912. Shortly afterward, Coffyn became the first pilot to fly under the Manhattan and Brooklyn bridges. (NASM)

140 After the Wrights, Glenn Curtiss was the most important name in American aviation in the pre–World War I period.

Thirty-one years old in 1909, Curtiss had just concluded a successful period of aeronautical experimentation with Bell's Aerial Experiment Association. He then teamed with cantankerous aviation pioneer Augustus Herring to form a company of their own. The Herring-Curtiss Company had the distinction of selling the first commercial aircraft in the United States, before the partnership was dissolved late in 1909, at which time Curtiss set out on his own. (CAM)

141 The first aircraft in the United States that could be called "commercial" was

named the *Gold Bug* (later, with an improved engine, the *Golden Flyer*) after the color of its fabric. Manufactured by Herring-Curtiss and sold to the Aeronautic Society of New York in June 1909, it set the basic design for most Curtiss aircraft over the next four years. Here it is seen during a test in Hammondsport, New York. (CAM)

142 Test-flying the *Gold Bug* at Morris Park in the Bronx, where the Aeronautic Society of New York conducted its activities up until mid-1909. (CAM)

142

143

144

145

143 Engaged by the Aeronautic Society as flying instructor, Curtiss felt he needed a larger space to fly his *Gold Bug.* He selected the open expanses of the Hempstead Plains at Mineola, Long Island, where the Aeronautic Society moved its headquarters and where Curtiss taught his first students and refined his own flying skills. (CAM)

144 On July 17, 1909, at Mineola, Curtiss in the *Gold Bug* won the *Scientific American* prize for the first flight of 25 kilometers. Based on this performance, Curtiss was selected to represent the United States at the upcoming Gordon Bennett Trophy races at Rheims, France. He won by sustaining a speed of 47 mph over 12.4 miles. (CAM)

146

145, 146 In the spring of 1910 Curtiss built a new machine, the *Albany Flyer* (seen here), which he used to attempt to win a $10,000 prize for the first flight between Albany and New York City. At 7:30 A.M. on May 29, the *Albany Flyer,* with a large float attached to its central skid, took off from a field near Albany. After one stop for refueling, Curtiss landed in New York at noon, having covered 137 miles in 2 hours, 32 minutes at an average speed of 54 mph. (NASM [145], CAM [146])

147 In 1911 the Curtiss Corporation introduced the Model "D." Some instances of this model had a forward elevator, others did not. All had ailerons mounted between the wings and most were powered by a 40- to 70-hp V-8 Curtiss engine. The Model D was sold to both civilian and military aviators and was frequently copied by amateur aircraft builders. Maneuverable, light and relatively fast, it was the most widely built type of plane in America before World War I. (CAM)

148

148   This closeup of a Curtiss Model D shows the unique shoulder-fork control system employed by Curtiss. The movable shoulder fork, above the seat, was connected to the ailerons by cables. As the pilot was sitting in the seat, the shoulder fork engaged his shoulders, and he turned the plane by simply leaning in the direction in which he wanted to go. The radiator may be seen directly behind the pilot's seat, and above this the fuel tank, attached to the underside of the wing. (CAM)

149   By far the most significant variant of the Curtiss Model D was the waterborne version—the hydroaeroplane. Most of the developmental work on this plane was done for the Navy at their base in San Diego in late 1910. On January 26, 1911, Curtiss made the first public flight taking off from and landing on water. His hydroaeroplane consisted essentially of a Model D with the addition of a large central float (just barely visible at the bottom of this photograph) in place of wheels and two outboard floats under the wings. Pleased with the flight results of this plane, the Navy ordered several in the spring of 1911. (CAM)

149

150   In the same year Curtiss produced an amphibious version called the "Triad," seen here, with wheels attached to the center float so the plane could operate off land or water. (CAM)

150

151

151   Late in 1911 Curtiss produced a sea-plane of the "flying boat" type, seen here. This differed from the earlier hydro-aeroplane in that it had a true hull rather than just added-on floats. This was also one of the few cases where Curtiss used a chain-drive system like those of the Wrights. Complications in this chain drive made this plane a failure and Curtiss made no attempt to develop this design any further. Nonetheless it was the first attempt to produce a true flying boat and valuable lessons were learned. (NASM)

152   The first successful flying boat was the Curtiss Model "E," developed in Hammondsport in 1912. Here, Glenn Curtiss and Henry Ford stand next to a Model E on Lake Keuka. Note the antiskid curtains along both sides of the engine bay. This aircraft was the first in a long line of flying boats, used for both military and civil applications, that made Curtiss famous. (CAM)

153   A Curtiss Model E flying low over Lake Keuka. The Model E was powered by 75- to 100-hp V-8 Curtiss engines and could reach a top speed of 50 mph. This early version had no "step" in the hull bottom, making it difficult to break contact with the surface of the water. (CAM)

152

153

154

155

156

154 The later version of the Model E, just taking off from the lake. This version had a stepped hull (invisible in this photo). (CAM)

155, 156 The Curtiss Model "F," the first truly practical flying boat, was by far the most successful of Curtiss' pre-war hydro-aeroplanes. A good many of them were produced for sportsmen as well as for the military. Here (**photo 155**) the stepped hull may be clearly seen. Note how the ailerons are still mounted between the wings as in Curtiss' earlier designs. (CAM)

157 In 1910, like the Wrights, Curtiss started his own touring exhibition company. One of his premier pilots was 21-year-old Beckwith Havens, seen here. Unsuccessful as an automobile salesman, Havens took $500 and went to Hammondsport for flying lessons, originally intending to be an airplane salesman. He gave up this idea when he found being on the exhibition circuit profitable. The early exhibition pilots had to contend with horrible flying fields and large, hostile crowds that often forced them to fly in dangerous winds. Most people were skeptical that an airplane could fly at all; when it did, they were amazed. (NASM)

158 Exhibition flying was a dangerous but lucrative career. Spectators increasingly demanded that pilots engage in hazardous stunts but, if successful, the pilots could earn up to a thousand dollars a day. Probably the most famous Curtiss exhibition pilot was the diminutive Charles K. Hamilton, seen here at age 24. Already experienced as a stunt parachutist and airship pilot, Hamilton always carried a loaded gun and was frequently drunk. He flew with a smoldering punk tied to a strut, from which he lit cigarettes. Hamilton quickly earned a reputation as the nerviest of all the early aviators. He survived 63 crashes and had two metal ribs as well as metal plates in his leg and skull. In June 1910 he won a $10,000 prize for a flight from New York to Philadelphia and back in a single day. At Belmont Park in October, he entertained the crowd with his trick landings—diving straight down from two hundred feet and pulling up five feet from the ground, straightening out and stopping right in front of the grandstand. Amazingly, Hamilton lived to age 28, at which time he died of—pneumonia! At that he lasted longer than most other early pilots, who died in nameless fields across America. (NASM)

157

158

Lincoln Beachey and his Aeroplane

159

159 The premier American stunt flier of the pre-World War I period was Lincoln Beachey, born in California in 1887. Beachey began his flying career with small dirigibles and in 1911 he earned his license with Curtiss. A short man who always flew in a business suit, Beachey was known for his specialty act of diving from 5,000 feet and pulling up at the last second to make a pinpoint landing. On June 27, 1911, he flew over Niagara's Horseshoe Falls and under the arch of the International Bridge down the gorge. In Chicago in that year he also set a new world altitude record of 11,573 feet. (CAM)

160 Beachey became widely known for a circus act that pitted his airplane against a race car driven by Barney Oldfield. The plane usually won. (NASM)

BARNEY OLDFIELD   LINCOLN BEACHEY

160

161 By 1912, Beachey was flying a specially built Curtiss, reinforced for acrobatics and powered by a rotary engine. In this plane on November 24, 1913, over San Diego, Beachey became the first American to "loop the loop." On March 14, 1915, Beachey was killed when the wings of his brand-new plane were torn off in a power dive over San Francisco Bay. (NASM)

162 The basic Curtiss Model D was certainly the most widely copied American aircraft of the pre-World War I period. Without benefit of plans, many small companies and individuals liberally copied its design. One such example is the Gammeter biplane, built in Akron, Ohio, in 1911, one of which is seen here with its new owner, James Lester Weeks of Long Island (in the checkered cap; at right is the Mr. Gammeter who designed the plane). (CAM)

161

162

163 A closeup of Weeks clearly shows the engaged shoulder-fork control and the push-rod for the forward elevator, attached directly to the control wheel. (CAM)

164 Weeks flying his Gammeter near Akron, ca. 1912. Atypically, Weeks lived to the age of 82, dying in 1972. (CAM)

165 John Moisant, who called himself "King of the Aviators," led a revolution in El Salvador and was a wealthy plantation owner prior to getting interested in aviation in 1909. After seeing and being excited by the Rheims Meet, Moisant built his own plane in France within three months. Moisant's plane, seen here, was unique in that it had an all-metal frame. However, it made only a short hop. Wanting to learn to fly, Moisant attended the Blériot school. After only four lessons, he purchased his own Blériot, and, on September 6, 1910, he became the first person to fly the English Channel with a passenger. In October 1910, he participated in the Belmont Park meet, where he won the race around the Statue of Liberty and back. (Two years later the honors were transferred retroactively to Claude Grahame-White; Moisant's victory had been challenged and he was disqualified for having started late.) Following the meet, John, along with his brother Alfred, formed a successful traveling flying circus. On December 31, 1910, however, Moisant was killed while attempting to set a new endurance record over New Orleans. Although his flying career was brief, for a while Moisant was an American hero. (NASM)

166 Thomas Baldwin, born in 1854, was one of the oldest of the early aviators. A former circus trapeze artist, he became interested in balloons and began to give parachuting exhibitions. In 1904 he built a very successful dirigible, the *California Arrow*, which was powered by an early Curtiss engine. (NASM)

167 In 1910 Baldwin built his own plane, the *Red Devil*, which was generally a copy of a Curtiss pusher with a Farman-type tail. So successful was this plane that Baldwin toured the country in it and never went back to flying airships. The *Red Devil* was powered by a 60-hp Hall-Scott engine and was unusual in that it had an all-metal frame. (NASM)

163

165

164

166

167

168

168   Among those who tested their own novel aerodynamic theories was Frank Boland of New York. At his workshop in Newark, New Jersey, Boland began experimenting with aircraft in 1908. By 1911 he had developed a unique tailless aircraft, seen here, which was powered by an engine of his own design and was flown successfully. He later developed a similar flying boat, in which he was killed in 1913. (CAM)

169   Clifford Harmon, a millionaire sportsman and balloonist, became interested in heavier-than-air flying machines in 1909. On August 20, 1910, flying his newly purchased Farman biplane, Harmon won the *Country Life in America* trophy for having made the first flight across Long Island Sound, from Garden City to Greenwich, covering 25 miles in 29 minutes. At the Harvard–Boston meet in September, Harmon won the prize for bomb dropping as well as for speed and duration. He later became the President of the Aero Club of America. (CAM)

170   Americans were generally behind the Europeans in the design of monoplanes at this time. The first successful American monoplane was the Type III of Dr. Henry Walden, a Long Island dentist. A member of the Aeronautic Society of New York starting in 1908, Walden developed two unsuccessful designs. His Type III, powered by an Anzani engine, first flew on December 9, 1909. Walden's most successful design was his Model IX, seen here at the Brighton Beach Race Track in Brooklyn. With this aircraft he participated in several air meets. (CAM)

171   Dr. Walden in his Model X at an air meet in St. Louis in 1911. (CAM)

172   It was recognized early on that aircraft could be very useful for aerial photography, both commercial and military. Here, *New York Herald Telegram* photographer Frank Dart, left, prepares to go aloft in a Wright aircraft from Long Island's Nassau Boulevard airfield in 1912. (CAM)

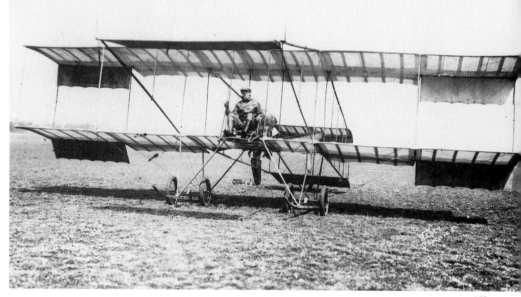

169

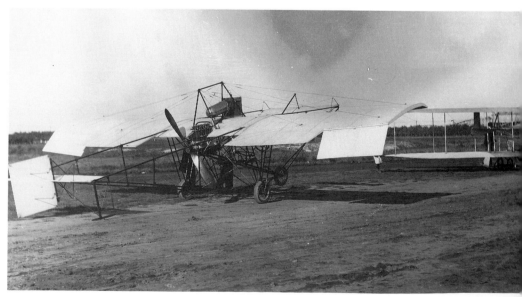

170

171

172

173

174

175

173–175 Arthur and Albert Heinrich, 23 and 21 years old, respectively, began building an aircraft of their own design in a chicken coop on their Baldwin, Long Island, farm in 1909. This plane, which first flew in May 1910, is historically important in that it was the first American monoplane powered by an American engine (60-hp Emerson boat engine). Both brothers flew the plane without benefit of flying lessons. The monoplane, of conventional construction, was also noteworthy in that it was among the first planes to employ modern-style ailerons. The airplane was also unique in that all control surfaces were attached to one combined wheel on a stick control column, allowing one-hand flying of the machine. Here, the Heinrich Model "A" can be seen under construction (**photo 173**), being moved to their flying field (**photo 174**) and ready to take off (**photo 175**). Notice that the person who spun the propeller is running in fright now that the engine has started. (CAM)

176 The Heinrich Model "D," seen here, was of a more advanced, streamlined design, which, nevertheless, reverted to using wing warping instead of ailerons. Up to 1917, the Heinrichs produced several planes of similar type as well as more advanced types. After that they remained in the aviation industry working for others as engineers. (CAM)

177 Arthur Heinrich is seen here in the rear cockpit of a Model D with Mrs. Mary Simms (later Mrs. Albert Heinrich) wearing typical period flying garb. (CAM)

176

177

178 Edson F. Gallaudet was a physics instructor at Yale University before leaving in 1908 to form his own aviation company. This is one of his first successful aircraft, the radically advanced Gallaudet Bullet of 1912. The aircraft was powered by a 100-hp Gnôme rotary engine buried in the nose of the plane and faired over with a streamlined mesh. A drive shaft connected the engine to the pusher propeller in the tail. Purportedly the aircraft was capable of speeds up to 100 mph. Unfortunately, injuries sustained in the crash of this aircraft on Long Island on July 24, 1912, cut short Gallaudet's flying career. He went on to sell aircraft of novel design to the U.S. Navy in the early 1920s. (CAM)

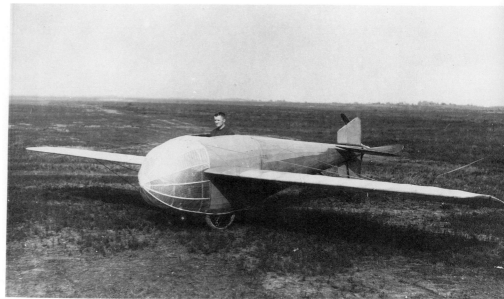

178

179 The first flight of a man-carrying powered aircraft in New England took place in Essex, Massachusetts, in February 1910, in a machine called the Herring-Burgess Number 1 (HB-1). W. Starling Burgess, a very successful yacht builder, had teamed up with the cantankerous Augustus Herring, formerly assistant to Octave Chanute and partner of Glenn Curtiss. Then Burgess and Herring produced a machine with some interesting features, the Herring-Burgess Number 2. This unique aircraft had eight triangular fins attached to the upper wing. Herring reasoned that if the machine tipped sideways, the force of the air against the fins would right it—thus giving it inherent lateral stability. The aircraft was also notable in that, like the original Wright Flyer, it was fitted with skids, not wheels. On April 17, 1910, this machine first flew near Ipswich, Massachusetts, with Herring himself at the controls. By June, however, Herring had left the company with a cash settlement in hand, and Burgess set up his own company. (CAM)

179

180 Herring-Burgess Number 3, seen here, was produced in May 1910, just before Herring left Herring-Burgess. First flown on May 14, the machine lacked the triangular fins of its predecessor, but, like the Number 2, it had no wheels. Built generally along Curtiss lines, this plane nevertheless relied on wing warping for control. In July, after Herring and Burgess had split up, the latter added both ailerons and wheels to the Number 3. In this form the aircraft competed at the Harvard–Boston air meet in September 1910. Though it failed to win any prizes, it attracted the attention of Wilbur Wright, who, impressed by its workmanship, suggested that the Burgess Company build Wright aircraft under license. (CAM)

180

181 By 1912 the Burgess Company was in fact building Wright biplanes under license. A former boat builder, Burgess fitted some of the Wright planes with pontoons, as seen here. Pleased with the results, Burgess then turned his attention to a new type of hydroaeroplane with an eye to attracting the attention of the U.S. Navy. (NASM)

182 Burgess became aware of the unique, inherently stable tailless biplane designed by John Dunne in England. In 1912 he obtained a license to build this type in America, soon manufactured as Burgess-Dunne aircraft. Burgess fitted the planes with central floats, as seen here, and he produced a number of these with two seats. One became Canada's first military aircraft, and several were purchased as the AH-7 by the U.S. Navy in 1914. (NASM)

181

182

183

184

186

183–185 Among monoplanes, the Blériot was the type most widely copied in America. The American Aeroplane Supply House (AASH), founded in Hempstead, Long Island, in late 1910, sold its first Blériot-type monoplane in 1911, went on to produce the first successful two-seat Blériots in this country and became the largest producer of monoplanes in America before World War I. Although AASH planes were fairly faithful copies of Blériot's designs, most were equipped with American-made Roberts engines. **Photo 183** shows one of their advertisements from late 1911 or early 1912. As stated, four basic models were offered: a single-seater, a two-seater, a racer and a military model, with prices ranging from $2,700 to $6,000. AASH also sold a great number of parts to individuals constructing their own Blériot copies all across America. **Photo 184** shows one of the two-seat versions on the Hempstead Plains airfield at Mineola, and **photo 185** is a view of the flying school they operated there. Hild and Marshonet were the company's founders. (CAM)

186 This Blériot-type plane was owned by George Nealy (left) of Stratford, Connecticut. Nealy purportedly experimented with gyroscopes on aircraft in an attempt to give them additional stability. In any event, this machine is powered by a three-cylinder Anzani engine. (CAM)

187–191 In April 1911 Alfred Moisant opened one of the first flying schools in America. Situated on the flat, treeless fields near Garden City, Long Island, the school boasted over a thousand unobstructed acres and excellent facilities. Widely considered an excellent school, Moisant's was the first to accept women, and the first licensed American women pilots were trained there. Moisant's program lasted a minimum of five weeks and cost $750, plus a $250 breakage deposit. The first week of the program consisted of ground school and covered the mechanics of flight. Moisant insisted that his students be knowledgeable with respect to the construction and repair of aircraft, including the engine. Thus, the second week covered airplane assembly and disassembly. The third week was spent using a primitive flight simulator, the fourth week flying a training plane that could rise no more than two or three feet (so students could master the controls). In the last week students flew solos under supervision in a variety of machines. Only Blériot aircraft were used, powered by 30- to 50-hp Gnôme engines. **Photo 187** shows a Moisant Blériot turning over the enormous flat expanse of the Hempstead Plains. In **photo 188**, an unknown student is seated in front of the Moisant hangar. In **photo 189**, chief instructor André Houpert checks the wind speed prior to a day's flying; if it was over 8 mph, they would not fly. **Photo 190** shows a lineup of Blériots on the flying field, **photo 191** the hangars belonging to the Moisant school. (CAM)

187

188

189

190

191

192

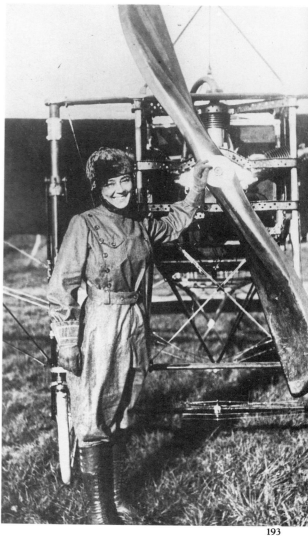

193

192 Harriet Quimby, a New York theater critic who was popular in high society, became enthusiastic about aviation after attending the 1910 air meet at Belmont Park, and she enrolled in the Moisant school shortly after it opened the following year. On August 11, 1911, she became the first licensed woman aviator in the United States. A beauty, she was admired by all who saw her in her striking purple flying outfit. She also proved to be a talented flier and she was asked to join the traveling Moisant exhibition team. In September 1911 she won a cross-country race at the Nassau Boulevard air meet, and then went on to tour the country putting on shows and participating in other air meets. She achieved stellar fame on April 16, 1912, when, in her new 50-hp Blériot, she became the first woman to fly the English Channel, flying almost entirely through clouds from Dover to Hardelot, south of Calais. After this she had her plane shipped to Boston, where she was to fare considerably less well. (NASM)

193 The second licensed woman pilot in America was Mathilde Moisant, sister of John and Alfred. On August 13, 1911, she passed her tests at her brother's school and immediately joined the Moisant exhibition team. At the Nassau Boulevard air meet in September she won the Rodman-Wanamaker trophy for having attained an altitude of 2,500 feet. On October 8, she was chased in her plane from airfield to airfield by several police cars as the authorities attempted to arrest her for flying on a Sunday. (The judge later let her off, saying there was no law against flying on any day.) By next spring, however, she gave up flying under intense pressure from her family, who had already lost her brother John to the dangerous pursuit. (NASM)

194 Harriet Quimby (right) and Mathilde Moisant in garb considerably more feminine than their flying gear. (NASM)

195 Bernetta Miller also received her license at the Moisant school, on September 25, 1912. She went on to join the Moisant Exhibition Flyers, and on October 1, 1912, at College Park, Maryland, she became the first person to demonstrate a monoplane before U.S. government officials. On January 20, 1913, while attempting to set a new women's altitude record, her oil line broke and she was covered with oil. Although partly blinded, she made a successful emergency landing. (CAM)

196 Ruth Law learned to fly at the Burgess Flying School in Boston in June 1912. She learned on a Wright aircraft, and when she purchased a Curtiss in 1913, she had it fitted with the Wright-type controls she was used to, seen here. On November 6, 1913, she became the first woman to fly at night, with a twenty-minute moonlight flight over Staten Island, New York. She continued to make exhibition flights around the country until 1919. (CAM)

194

195

196

197–199 Blanche Stuart Scott was the first American woman to make a solo flight, on September 2, 1910. She had been personally taught to fly by Glenn Curtiss as a favor to a friend, and she was not a regular pupil at his school (neither he nor the Wrights admitted women). Scott made her public debut with the Curtiss Exhibition Team in Chicago in October 1910 (**photo 197**). The following year she gave exhibition flights all over the country, performing aerobatic tricks like inverted flight, flying under bridges and vertical power dives from altitude. In **photo 198** she is seen flying a Glenn Martin biplane (basically a copy of a Curtiss) at Dominguez field near Los Angeles in 1912. In 1913 she began flying Baldwin's *Red Devil* (**photo 199**), in which she was injured in a crash in May. She flew on and off until 1916, when she retired, feeling a strong aversion to the public's morbid interest in crashes. She had never received a pilot's license. (CAM)

200 In 1912, Alys McKey became the first woman pilot who was a native of the West. She learned to fly—in response to an ad looking for a woman pilot for an exhibition team—on the same old Curtiss plane that had been used on the flight down the Hudson in 1909. McKey first soloed in November 1912. In her Curtiss Model D, seen here, she was the first woman to fly over Washington, Oregon and Idaho. In August 1913, she also became the first woman to fly over Canada. She later became a flight instructor, even though she had never had a license. (CAM)

197

198

199

200

201 Katherine Stinson was the oldest in a family of four prominent aviators and the fourth woman in the United States to obtain a pilot's license, qualifying on July 24, 1912, in a Wright Model B (seen here; her instructor, Max Lillie, is at the left), after having learned to fly at the Lillie school near Chicago. She was only 16 years old! Between 1913 and 1916 Stinson toured the United States, performing in flying exhibitions at meets and fairs. In July 1915 she became the first woman to loop the loop (near Chicago). In 1916 she established a flying school near San Antonio, Texas, and during World War I she toured the country in a Curtiss JN raising money for the Red Cross. While traveling in Europe at the end of the war she contracted influenza; subsequently, ill health forced her to retire from aviation. (CAM)

202 Pioneer aviator and inventor Lawrence Sperry built his first aircraft in 1911, seen here at the Sheepshead Bay Speedway in Brooklyn. This unique plane had spars mounted on top of the wing and an all-moving tail. Sperry, who had received no formal training, taught himself to fly this aircraft. (CAM)

203 Realizing he needed proper instruction, Sperry earned his flying license in Hammondsport, soloing on the Curtiss Model D, in which he is seen here, in 1912. (CAM)

204 With the help of his inventor/manufacturer father, Elmer Sperry, Lawrence Sperry went on to develop the turn-and-bank indicator, retractable landing gear and, most important, the automatic pilot, seen here as installed in a Curtiss flying boat early in 1914. (CAM)

205 Lawrence Sperry's automatic pilot, called by him the "gyro-stabilizer," was a revolutionary invention and won him a 50,000-franc prize from the French government. This photo shows him demonstrating it in his Curtiss F flying boat at the prize competition in Bezons, France, on July 3, 1914. His mechanic stood on the wing, as seen here, and Sperry removed his hands from the controls, yet the plane continued its steady flight. Sperry's gyro-stabilizer was the direct ancestor of all the automatic pilots of today. Sperry died young in a tragic accident in 1923, when a light plane of his own design (a "Messenger") crashed in the English Channel. (CAM)

201

202

203

204

205

206

207

206–210 The first great international air meet, known as *La Grande Semaine d'Aviation de la Champagne,* was held at Rheims, in the Champagne region of France, from August 22 to August 29, 1909. During this week more new records were set daily than at any meet since. A watershed event in aviation history, it did a great deal to popularize mechanical flight and made heroes of the first aviators. Racing pylons, tents, wooden hangars, a huge scoreboard and an enormous covered grandstand were specially constructed for the event. The weather was generally good, and enormous, enthusiastic crowds (over 500,000 people) were drawn daily. Virtually none of these spectators had ever seen an airplane in flight and they were truly awed by the sight. A total of 200,000 francs was offered in prize money, with the largest and most prestigious prize being offered for the first annual running of the James Gordon Bennett speed race. Thirty-eight aircraft competed at the meet, many of them flown by the world's leading aviators. The majority were French, Glenn Curtiss begin the only American. Surprisingly, the Wright brothers declined to attend, although six Wright-type aircraft were flown, one of which may be seen passing the stands in **photo 206**. The crowds were certainly treated to a spectacle. In a typical scene, **photo 207** shows four planes in the air at once; at times up to ten machines could be seen in the air at the same time. At one point, unfortunately, twelve machines could also be seen wrecked on the ground at the same time. **Photo 208** shows the magnificent Antoinette in which Hubert Latham won prizes for altitude and distance. Eugène Lefebvre, flying a Wright (**photo 209**), put on a spectacular show of aerobatics with his tight, low-altitude turns, but he failed to get more than 35 mph out of his plane, putting him out of the running for any speed prizes. The greatest surprise by far was the appearance of Glenn Curtiss in a modified *Golden Flyer* with a new 50-hp engine (**photo 210**). The machine was prepared in less than four weeks, and Curtiss had virtually no time to test it, arriving only hours before the qualifying trials were held. As he had only one plane and one engine, Curtiss did virtually no flying before the Gordon Bennett speed race near the end of the meet. Then, on August 28, Curtiss flew the two-lap, 20-kilometer race at a speed of 47 mph, narrowly defeating Blériot, the favorite, by only six seconds. This was truly a day of glory for the United States, and Curtiss was instantly catapulted to stardom. Following Rheims, Curtiss went to another meet in Brescia, Italy, where he again won the grand prize. He then returned to the United States to prepare a new machine for an upcoming meet in Los Angeles. (NASM)

208

209

210

211

213

212

211 From January 10 to 20, 1910, America's first air meet took place at the Dominguez Ranch south of Los Angeles. Although not a truly major meet, it had a variety of contests, including those for speed, altitude, endurance, accurate landing, bomb dropping, weight carrying and cross-country flight. Such events helped the progress of aviation by spurring development of better engines, refined aerodynamics and more efficient control systems. Frenchman Louis Paulhan won the prizes for altitude (4,164 feet) and endurance (64 miles in 1 hour 50 minutes), while Glenn Curtiss set a new mark for speed with a passenger at 55 mph. Curtiss brought his entire team to this meet, including Clifford Harmon, Charles K. Hamilton, Frank Johnson and his first stu-

dent, Frank Willard, seen in this photo. (NASM)

212, 213 Several aerial exhibitions were held around the country in 1910 and 1911. These were different from contest meets in that the aviators were paid to put on an exhibition; they did not compete for prizes. One of the more notable of such exhibitions was held at the Sheepshead Bay Speedway in Brooklyn from August 19 to 21, 1910. Although such events usually drew only local talent, this one did attract Curtiss, J. A. D. McCurdy, Frank Willard and "Bud" Mars, another of Curtiss' associates. In **photo 212**, crowds gather around a Wright Model B; in **photo 213**, a Farman soars above the spectators. (CAM)

214

215

216

214, 215 In September an air meet organized by the newly formed Harvard Aeronautical Society was held near Boston. Both Wilbur Wright and Glenn Curtiss attended (**photo 214** shows a Curtiss biplane), but the real star was Claude Grahame-White (seen in his Farman biplane in **photo 215**), who had gladly accepted $50,000 plus expenses to appear and won prizes for speed, accurate landing, distance flying and bomb dropping. During the course of the meet he was also paid up to $500 to fly wealthy socialites around the field. Large summer crowds—and even President William Howard Taft—attended. Grahame-White offered the Chief Executive a ride but the 300-pound Taft declined. (NASM)

216, 217 From October 22 to 30, 1910, Belmont Park Race Track, just outside of New York City, was the site of an International Aviation Tournament that far surpassed anything yet seen in the United States. A total of $72,300 in prize money was offered, and 27 aviators from several countries participated, including the Wright brothers' team (the Wrights attended but did not themselves participate), the team of Glenn Curtiss (who also did not personally participate), John Moisant, Thomas Baldwin, Alfred Leblanc, Hubert Latham and Claude Grahame-White. The weather on opening day could scarcely have been worse. Steady rain persisted throughout the day, killing ignition systems and generally making flight impossible. Rather than disappoint the faithful (about a thousand people showed up), a few aviators did make short flights, such as Grahame-White, seen in these photos in his Blériot among the puddles. (CAM)

218 The weather at Belmont Park improved after the miserable opening day, and enormous crowds came by train, automobile and bicycle—and on foot—to witness the miracle of powered flight. Among the spectators were not only the average person but also the elite of New York society. Daily newspapers each devoted several pages to coverage of the meet, and people fought to be near the godlike aviators, despite the hazard even to spectators. The racing course was dangerous and tight, with many obstacles. One corner, dubbed "dead man's turn," allowed only 100 feet of space between a pylon and the grandstand. Here a Curtiss Model D soars past the thrilled crowd. (CAM)

219 Britain's James Radley sails past the scoreboard in his Blériot. Of the spectators at Belmont Park, the few who had actually seen an aircraft before were probably familiar with the American biplanes of Wright and Curtiss. The Europeans provided an interesting contrast with their Blériot, Antoinette and Demoiselle monoplanes. (NASM)

217

218

219

220

221

220 At one point on October 24 a total of ten machines could be seen in the air at once, drawing a storm of applause from the crowd. Here Hubert Latham, who thrilled New Yorkers with his graceful handling of his Antoinette, leads Ralph Johnstone in his Wright Model B. Johnstone was to duel teammate Arch Hoxsey daily to set new altitude records. (NASM)

221 The new Farman biplane of wealthy American sportsman Clifford Harmon in its hangar. (CAM)

222 Here Harmon is shown seated in his plane. Glenn Curtiss stands at the left. Harmon, who had been the first to fly across Long Island Sound two months earlier, did not fare well at Belmont, as his plane crashed and was destroyed. (CAM)

223 The Blériot of Count Jacques de Lesseps revs up in front of "Hangar Row" at Belmont. Twenty hangars and four huge tents had been specially constructed for this air meet. (CAM)

222

223

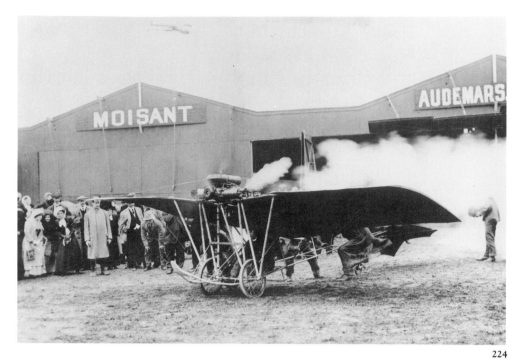

224

224 At Belmont Roland Garros warms up his tiny Demoiselle, which came to be nicknamed "The Infuriated Grasshopper." Though Garros won nothing at Belmont, he went on to become the first "ace" of World War I. (CAM)

225

225 One of the two major events at the Belmont Park meet was the second running of the Gordon Bennett speed race, on October 29. England's Grahame-White in his racing Blériot was favored to win as Glenn Curtiss refused to participate. American hopes were pinned on Walter Brookins flying a Wright Model "R," known as the "Baby Grand." This small machine with only a 21-foot wingspan was powered by an eight-cylinder 60-hp engine. (NASM)

226 When Alfred Leblanc crashed during his speed run, Brookins flew over to investigate, lost control and abruptly spun in to a crash from 50 feet. Brookins was unhurt but the Baby Grand was effectively out of the running. Grahame-White won the trophy with a speed of 61.3 mph. (NASM)

226

227

228

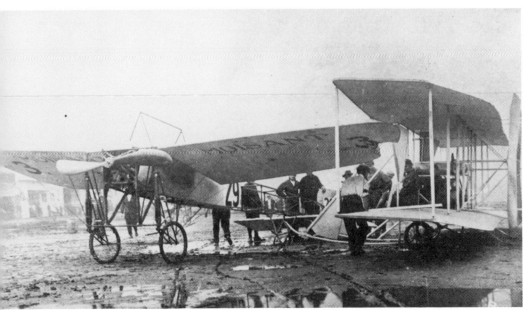

229

227 For most people, the key event of the Belmont Park meet was the Statue of Liberty race, a flight of 34 dangerous miles across land and sea, from Belmont Park around the Statue of Liberty and back. Since this event was held on a Sunday, October 30, the devout Wrights refused to let their planes fly. Once again, Grahame-White was the favorite and he flew a fast but indirect route, skirting the Brooklyn shoreline. American hopes seemed to fade entirely when their only entrant, John Moisant, rammed into Harmon's plane while trying to take off. (NASM)

228 Not to be deterred, Moisant offered Alfred Leblanc, who had been injured, $10,000 for his spare Blériot (far more than the machine was worth) in a desperate attempt to retain national honor in a race around our national symbol. The sporting Leblanc accepted the offer, and Moisant immediately took off with the wet paint of his number trailing down the fuselage. For the next half hour the gathered throng (as seen here) waited silently, straining for a glimpse of the returning aviator and insistently checking their watches. In an effort to beat Grahame-White, Moisant flew a shorter but more dangerous route, directly across the heart of populous Brooklyn. After the speck of his plane had reappeared on the horizon and he crossed the finish line, the judges announced that Moisant had beaten Grahame-White's time—by just one minute. Pandemonium swept the field, people hugged each other and threw hats in the air. Moisant was carried from the field wrapped in an American flag—we had acquired a new national hero. (Ironically, Moisant was later disqualified—he had started too late! The prize went to Grahame-White after all.) (NASM)

229 The International Aviation Meet in Chicago in August 1911 was a big, wild exhibition that saw one new record set—and two pilots killed. The Wright team sent a total of twelve pilots, but the smaller Curtiss crew stole the show, as when Lincoln Beachey, having added an extra ten-gallon fuel tank to his little Curtiss pusher, coaxed it to a record 11,642 feet. This was also the first meet at which England's future legend Thomas Sopwith appeared. By the time the meet was over, the prize for the most air time went to newcomer Cal Rodgers. The photo records the collision of Alfred Moisant's Blériot with Frank Coffyn's Wright on the ground—a reminder of just how hard to control on the ground pre–World War I aircraft were, lacking as they did steerable wheels or brakes. (NASM)

230

231

232

230 From September 23 to 30, 1911, Long Island was the site of another air tournament, the International Aviation Meet at the Nassau Boulevard Aerodrome in Garden City. Although no major flying records were broken at this meet, a record number of aviators participated—36 from several countries, with over 60 planes. This was also the first major air meet in which women (four of them) competed with men. Here, Army Lieutenant H. H. Arnold (the same "Hap" Arnold who went on to command the U.S. Army Air Corps) turns his Burgess-Wright machine over the field. (CAM)

231 George H. Beatty flies his Wright Model B in the passenger-carrying contest. (CAM)

232 H. H. Brown skims the field in his Wright. Note the horse-drawn wagons in the rear—a reminder of how long ago this was. (CAM)

233 Harry N. Atwood at the controls of his Burgess-Wright. Atwood won the scouting contest by locating some Army men hidden in some nearby woods—a portent of the future wartime use of airplanes. (CAM)

234 Lt. Arnold rounds a pylon alongside Britain's Tommy Sopwith. Both are flying Wright machines. (CAM)

235 A closeup of Tommy Sopwith in his Wright at Nassau Boulevard. Sopwith, who won several contests at the meet, went on to build some of the greatest planes in aviation history. (CAM)

233

234

235

236

237

236, 237   An aviator at the controls of Clifford Harmon's Farman (**photo 236**) and (at right in **photo 237**) Harmon passing the time with Glenn Curtiss at the Nassau Boulevard meet. (CAM)

238   Hélène Dutrieu of France flew her Farman biplane several times at the meet but did not win any prizes. (CAM)

239, 240   A speedy Deperdussin monoplane (**photo 239**) and a closeup of its Anzani engine. (CAM)

238

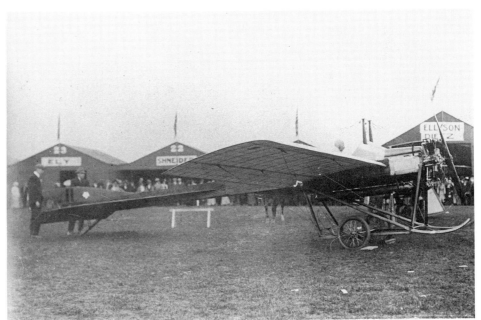

239

240

241

242

241 Claude Grahame-White in his new plane, the "Baby Grahame-White," at Nassau Boulevard. This new machine, supposed to be inherently stable, was a two-seat pusher biplane introduced in late 1910. The wings were each made in three sections for easy land transport. It was also fitted with a very rigid undercarriage. (CAM)

242 James V. Martin, an eccentric pioneer of early aviation, flew his new biplane, built by the Queen Aeroplane Company, at the Nassau Boulevard meet. Martin flew this machine several times but failed to win any prizes. He ended his career building automobiles. (CAM)

243

244

245

243–245 By far the most important event of the Nassau Boulevard meet was the first official carrying of the U.S. mail by air, on September 23, 1911. **Photo 243** shows pilot Earle Ovington handing a sack of mail to Postmaster General Frank Hitchcock on September 25. As there was so little room in the cockpit of his American-made Blériot, Ovington carried the mail on his lap for the three-mile flight to a prearranged spot near the Mineola Post Office. Obviously these pioneering flights were for demonstration purposes only, but they did show the potential of the airplane. **Photo 244** shows the airmail station at the Nassau Boulevard Aerodrome, and **photo 245** Ovington flying over the mail station headed toward Mineola. (CAM)

246
247

246, 247   This American-made Queen monoplane of Blériot type was flown by Earle Ovington (seen here) to deliver the mail, though not on the historic first flight. Later at the Nassau Boulevard meet it was flown by Dr. Charles Clarke, who crashed it and lost his life. (CAM)

248, 249   In March of 1912, the first international meet for hydroaeroplanes was held in Monaco. While this meet demonstrated no big breakthroughs, it did reveal the comparative safety in flying planes over water. The crowds got to witness the spectacle of five machines deliberately being crashed into the sea, as seen here with Paul Rúgere and his Voisin "Canard." Many paying passengers were carried without mishap. (NASM)

248
249

250

250–254 As part of a California aviation meet in 1910, William Randolph Hearst offered a $50,000 prize for the first transcontinental flight made in 30 days or less. In September 1911, three brave aviators attempted to claim the prize. Robert Fowler began from San Francisco but was forced to quit when the windy heights of the Sierras proved to be too much for his frail Wright. James Ward started from New York in his Curtiss Model D but he gave up after a crash in upstate New York. By far the most determined entrant was Calbraith Rodgers **(photo 250)**, who had secured the backing of the Armour Corporation, which financed the flight in return for Rodgers' promotion of Armour's new grape soda, "Vin Fiz," after which the specially built Wright "EX" biplane was named. Armour saw to it that a special train followed Rodgers carrying enough spare parts to keep repairing his plane en route. Even with this assistance, it was an extremely hazardous endeavor. Rodgers had no navigational equipment, there were no landing fields along the way, and no advance weather reports were avail-

able. In fact the Wright machine would be pushed to its limits by the harsh conditions of the journey. On September 17, 1911, Rodgers took off from Sheepshead Bay Speedway near the Atlantic Ocean in New York (**photos 251 and 252**) heading west toward the Pacific and his destiny. What followed over the next 49 days is remembered as one of the great feats of human perseverance and courage. Rodgers survived 14 crashes (which were due mostly to primitive landing fields; the results of two are shown in **photos 253 and 254**), an exploding engine, thunderstorms, souvenir hunters, even an attack by an eagle. He finally reached Pasadena, California, on November 5, too late to claim the Hearst prize but satisfied that he had demonstrated the potential of the airplane. His actual flying time had been 3 days, 10 hours, 4 minutes. On December 10 he actually dipped the wheels of the *Vin Fiz* in the waters of the Pacific Ocean. Sadly, not 500 feet from that spot at Long Beach, Rodgers was killed in a plane crash on April 3, 1912, only a few months later. (NASM)

252

253

254

255

256

257

255–259   In the early years of flight, for every successful aircraft there was a far greater number of failures. This was largely because so little was known about aerodynamics, lift, control, etc. In this vacuum of knowledge, anyone with any sort of wild idea felt justified in simply building an airplane to try it out. As ridiculous as these early aviators look now, it was through such trial-and-error experimentation that the successful aircraft was born and matured. The five planes pictured here, built in the 1906–1909 period by forgotten experimenters, are a monument—but a small percentage of the failures that occurred on the way to success. (NASM)

258

260

260 Gustave White's last airplane, the Beach-Whitehead biplane, seen here, was built near Stratford, Connecticut, in 1908. Whitehead, who claimed to have flown as early as 1901, sits at the wheel. The Whitehead-designed engine drove two propellers by means of flat belts from a large wooden wheel. A crude design, this plane never flew. (CAM)

261 The Kimball helicopter, built in 1908 by Wilbur R. Kimball of the Aeronautic Society of New York, had 20 propellers and a 50-hp engine. Still, these failed to lift it off the ground. (CAM)

262 Kimball's second machine, a biplane with eight cable-driven propellers powered by a single engine, was built in 1909. It also failed to fly. (CAM)

261

262

263 Morris Bokor's triplane was also built under the auspices of the Aeronautic Society of New York. This machine actually won a $500 cash prize for excellence of construction (independent of performance), the first money prize ever won by a flying machine in America. Nevertheless this plane too failed to leave the ground. (CAM)

263

264

264, 265 This biplane designed by Franz Miller of Turin for Mario Cobianchi was among the first aircraft built in Italy. It featured rudders mounted between the plane's wings and an upper wing that had a negative dihedral and was uncovered in the middle. Although it managed a brief bounce into the air in September 1909, it was not successful. (CAM)

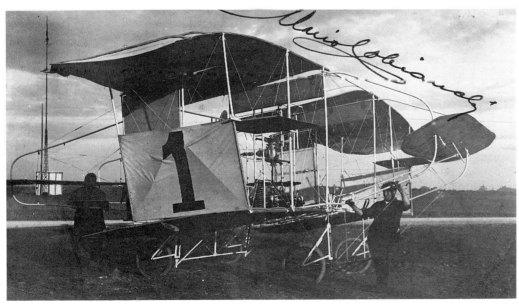

265

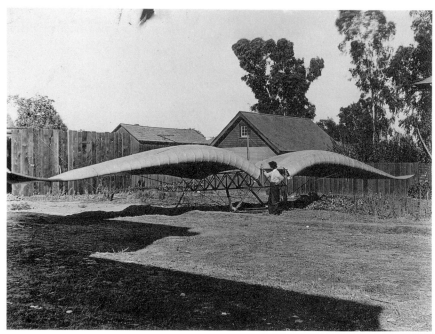

266

267

268

266 This aircraft with highly curved wings, patterned after those of a gull, was designed and built in 1910 by L. F. Burke of Philadelphia. It never flew. (CAM)

267 Professor J. S. Zerbes' bizarre multiplane, seen here at Dominguez airfield near Los Angeles in 1910, failed to rise from the ground. (CAM)

268 The Geary circular triplane, seen on the Hempstead Plains airfield in August 1911. This plane was also unsuccessful. (CAM)

269 The McCormick-Dietz paraplane at the Nassau Boulevard Aerodrome in 1911. The tube in the center was said to contain a parachute—never needed, since the plane never left the ground. (CAM)

269

270

271

270, 271 The Fity Monoplane at Nassau Boulevard in the fall of 1911. Fity developed this plane with folding wings so it could be driven on a road. It was said to have made three brief hops before crashing. (CAM)

272 The García Polyplane, seen at the Nassau Boulevard Aerodrome in 1912, was built by Zoilo García and was the first airplane built by a Dominican. It was not successful. (CAM)

273, 274 The wings of this twelve-winged plane built by Howard Huntington in Hollis, Queens, New York, in 1912, were most likely inspired by the wings of seagulls. Although this plane never flew, in 1914 Huntington built a much smaller plane with only two wings, also inspired by gulls, that did fly. (CAM)

272

273

274

THE PRICE

275 Fatal airplane crashes were very common in the 1909–1913 period (before then most planes couldn't get off the ground!). This was the result of a number of factors. The aircraft were frail, easily upset by the slightest gust of wind, and structural failures were not uncommon. Pilots pushed these planes to their limits, even though the best of these planes had limited means of being controlled. Pilots generally wore no crash helmets or seat belts. The current thinking was that it would be safer to be thrown free of the crash. In many cases, however, the pilot was not thrown free anyway, and the proximity of the engine made it more likely that he would be crushed in a crash. Pilots in those days paid a high price for their glory. As terrible as this price was, however, the great number of crashes in this period ultimately led to the development of safer aircraft—an evolution that continues today. This photo shows the crash of the Aerial Experiment Association's *White Wing* in 1908. (NASM)

276 The wreck of Louis Breguet's plane at the Rheims meet, 1909. (NASM)

275

277   The wreck of a Voisin at the same meet, 1909. (CAM)

278   The wreck of Louis Blériot's plane, also at Rheims, 1909. (CAM)

279   Another crash of a Breguet biplane at Rheims, 1909.

280   The wreck of Eugène Lefebvre's Wright biplane, 1909. (CAM)

281   W. R. Kimball about to crash in his glider at Morris Park, Bronx, New York, 1909. (CAM)

277

278

279

280

281

282

283

282   The Heinrich monoplane after a crash at the Hempstead Plains field, 1909. (CAM)

283   The wreck of an Antoinette at Heliopolis, Egypt, 1910. (CAM)

284   The wreck of Georges Chavez's Farman at Nice, April 17, 1910. (CAM)

284

285 Cavalrymen and other spectators view the remains of the Voisin in which the Baronne Raymonde de Laroche crashed at Rheims, France, in 1910. Although the accident was nearly fatal, Laroche, remarkably, survived. (CAM)

286 Charles Wachter falling to his death on July 3, 1910, after the wing of his Antoinette collapsed in flight. (CAM)

287 Ralph Johnstone's fatal crash in Denver, November 17, 1910. (NASM)

285

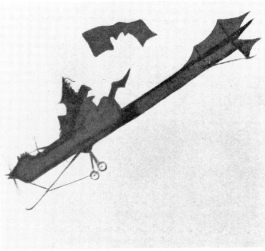

286

287

288

288   Arch Hoxsey plunging to his death in Los Angeles, December 31, 1910. (CAM)

289   The result of an encounter of a Voisin with a telephone pole in 1911. Note the telephone lines at the bottom in the photo. Remarkably, French pilot Legal survived. (CAM)

290   The crash of the Curtiss biplane of James Lester Weeks on the Hempstead Plains in 1911. When Weeks was asked why he soon stopped flying, he replied, "I was spending too much time in hospitals." (CAM)

291   Harriet Quimby's fatal crash in Boston Harbor, July 1, 1912. (NASM)

292   The overturned wreckage of a Curtiss flying boat is hoisted out of Lake Keuka, New York, in 1912. (CAM)

289

290

291

292

293

294

293 The development of the airplane originally occurred in peacetime, and few people, especially at a governmental level, were farsighted enough to envision its military uses. In the United States, the Army, after a long delay, finally acknowledged that the flying machine might be of use for scouting (the fighters and bombers of World War I, into which the earlier machines would quickly evolve, were foreseen by almost no one even on the eve of the war), and a Model A Wright airplane was ordered as "Signal Corps. No. 1" on August 2, 1909. The Model B, seen here, followed in 1911. (NASM)

294 In 1911 the Navy ordered its first airplanes, one of which was a Wright Model "B-1" hydroaeroplane (essentially a pontoon-mounted version of the Model B), for which they paid $5,000. This machine, seen here, was delivered in Annapolis on July 19. By the fall of the following year, the Navy was flying several Wright Model "B-2" hydroaeroplanes at its North Island, San Diego, training base. (NASM)

295 The first hesitant experiments in aerial gunnery were undertaken in the summer of 1910. This drawing, made in August, shows Glenn Curtiss flying Lt. Jacob Fickel of the 29th Infantry over the Sheepshead Bay Speedway, Brooklyn, New York. From an altitude of 100 feet, Lt. Fickel fired his Springfield rifle at a white target on the ground, scoring one hit. This initial attempt at aerial gunnery proved that there was no danger that the recoil of the gun would affect the balance of the plane. (CAM)

296 Also in the summer of 1910, Thomas Baldwin flying his *Red Devil* made the first experiment in air-to-air gunnery. At the Hempstead Plains field in Mineola, Baldwin took aloft local trapshooter William Simonson, who fired at tins cans thrown from the ground. Simonson was able to hit about half of the cans. In this photo he can be seen firing over Baldwin's shoulder from a temporary seat rigged behind the pilot. (CAM)

295

296

297

297–299 On November 14, 1910, Curtiss exhibition pilot Eugene Ely (**photo 297**) roared down a temporary wooden deck on the U.S.S. *Birmingham*, anchored in Hampton Roads, Virginia. After lifting off (**photo 298**), though Ely came perilously close to the water, he was able to fly successfully the two and a half miles to shore and land safely, thus completing the first airplane flight made from the deck of a ship. Two months later, on January 18, 1911, Ely accomplished the same feat in reverse. After taking off from the Presidio military base in San Francisco, he flew out over San Francisco Bay and safely alighted on a temporary 128-foot-long wooden deck on the U.S.S. *Pennsylvania* (**photo 299**). Then Ely had lunch with the captain and flew back to San Francisco. With these pioneering flights, the aircraft carrier was born. (NASM [297, 298], CAM [299])

300 The first experiments with live bombs dropped from aircraft were carried out in early 1911 by Army Lt. M. S. Crissy in San Francisco. Philip O. Parmalee is the pilot of this Wright Model B. (CAM)

298

299

300

301

302

301 Whereas the Army had purchased its first airplane in 1909, the Navy, understandably, waited until a suitable hydroaeroplane could be developed, although they were impressed with the promising flights of Eugene Ely. Glenn Curtiss was the first aviation pioneer to work closely with the Navy, and it was he who developed the first hydroaeroplane and trained the first Navy pilots (four of them), in San Diego in 1911. In July, the Navy ordered its first planes, two of which were Curtiss A-1's (the third was a Wright B-1 [see photo 294]). The Curtiss A-1, shown here, was used for many Naval experiments, and variations of this model were ordered by the Navy as late as 1915. (CAM)

302 By the end of 1912, the Navy was ordering more advanced aircraft from Curtiss, like this "C"-series flying boat. These were powered by 90- to 100-hp OX-5 engines, featured greatly improved hull designs and could carry a crew of two. First delivered the following year, they cost the government $6,350 each. They were generally flown out of the Navy's Pensacola, Florida, base. (CAM)

303 By 1913 the airplane had evolved sufficiently that the modern warplane, such as were massively used in World War I, could be seen to be taking shape. Such now-strange-looking types as the canard (tail-first) planes were gone, and all warplanes had tractor propellers (the opposite of the pusher—rear-mounted—propellers used on all early Wright and many other pioneering aircraft). In 1912, the first bombsights were developed, and military men had begun to think about ways to mount on planes guns that would fire straight ahead. This and the next two photos show some of the most advanced military aircraft of 1913. The Curtiss Model "G" "Scout" seen here, was the first tractor-type military aircraft built by Curtiss. Sold to the Signal Corps for $5,500 in April 1913, it was an immediate predecessor of the famous Curtiss "Jenny" of World War I and after. (NASM)

303

304

306

307

304 An Avro 504, first flown in July 1913. Ten thousand were sold to the Royal Flying Corps and the Royal Navy from then through 1920. (CAM)

305 A Sopwith "Tabloid," capable of achieving a speed of 92 mph. Substantial numbers were built for the Royal Flying Corps and the Royal Navy between 1913 and 1915. This was a direct predecessor of the Sopwith "Camel" of World War I fame. (NASM)

306 The shape of things to come. By 1915 virtually all military aircraft were equipped with machine guns. Just a few short years earlier the airplane had been a contraption for dreaming tinkerers, a medium for daredevil aerial showmen and -women, and a toy of the rich. Now it had become a grim tool of wartime destruction, in which role it has continued to the present day. (CAM)

307 What the pioneers hoped would never happen: as the first bombs of military aircraft rained down on civilians, the airplane—once called the "messenger of peace"—was now regarded as yet one more implement of destruction. (CAM)

INDEX

Note: *Italic references to roman numerals indicate pages; all other references are to captions.*